second-act careers

second-act careers

50+ ways to profit from your passions during **semi-retirement**

NANCY COLLAMER, MS

TEN SPEED PRESS
Berkeley

Ten Speed Press and the Ten Speed Press colophon are registered trademarks
of Random House, Inc.

Library of Congress Cataloging-in-Publication Data
Collamer, Nancy, 1957-
 Second-act careers : 50+ ways to profit from your passions during semi-
retirement / Nancy Collamer.—1st ed.
    p. cm.
 Includes index.
 1. Career changes. 2. Retirees—Employment. I. Title.
 HF5384.C65 2013
 650.14086′96—dc23

ISBN 978-1-60774-382-8
eISBN 978-1-60774-383-5

Printed in the United States of America

Cover design by Katy Brown
Interior design by Colleen Cain

10 9 8 7 6 5 4 3 2 1

First Edition

Contents

PART TWO

CREATING YOUR SECOND-ACT CAREER **184**

Acknowledgments

This book would never have happened without the encouragement of my wonderful literary agent, Marilyn Allen. Marilyn, thank you for your friendship and belief in the importance of this book. I am so thrilled that we finally got the chance to work together! To the team at Ten Speed Press—in particular my editor, Sara Golski—thank you for your warm welcome, savvy advice, and editorial assistance. I am truly honored to be part of the Ten Speed family.

One of the aspects I enjoy most about my job is that I get to work in a profession filled with warm, smart, and supportive colleagues—and a few deserve special mention. To my "lunch bunch"—Karen Kirchner, Susan Gannon, and Linsey Levine—thank you for more than a decade of support, brainstorming, and wonderful holiday luncheons. Linsey, it was indeed serendipitous that we earned our master's degrees at the same time; you have been my personal "career counsel" on more occasions than I care to admit. To Susan Joyce of Job-hunt.org, thanks for showcasing me on your site; and to my accountability buddies, Shannon White and Pat Katepoo, much *mahalo* for keeping me focused, on track, and productive—at least most of the time!

To the best clients in the world, thank you for allowing me to be part of your journey; you have inspired me with your brilliance and honored me with your trust. This book would never have been possible without you. And to all the remarkable people who agreed to be interviewed for this book, thank you for being so generous with your time, insights, and willingness to share your personal stories.

Much gratitude is also due to all my friends, gym buddies, UNC pals, Shir Ami supporters, and neighbors who have taken such great interest in this project. Your enthusiasm and "How are you holding up?" phone calls kept me going day after day.

A very special thank-you to my brother, David Jarmul, and his wife, Champa, for your brainstorming help and advice; and to my sister, Ruth Jarmul, and her husband, Irv Rosenthal, for your unfailing encouragement, love, and support. I am truly blessed to have such wonderful siblings. My one regret in writing this book is that our parents, Seymour and Lore Jarmul, are not alive to see this book in print. I was raised in a family of authors, and I know they would have been delighted to know I have joined their ranks. Thank you Mom and Dad for everything— I truly could not have asked for better role models.

To my two delightful daughters, Danielle and Juliana, who encouraged and cheered me every step of this journey, thank you for making me one proud "Nin." You enrich my life beyond measure, and I love you more than words can say.

And last, but never ever least, to my amazing husband, Joel Collamer: thanks for thirty-plus years of love, listening, and laughter. I know it sounds clichéd to say this wouldn't have been possible without your support, but it's true. Thank you for believing in me, cooking for me (although I've had enough of the cheese, thank you), entertaining me with your antics, and for being my best friend. This book is dedicated to you, with my love, thanks, and gratitude.

Second-Act Careers

Introduction

When I told people that I was writing a book about semi-retirement careers, I wasn't quite sure if people would understand what I meant. After all, by definition, "working during retirement" is an oxymoron. But I quickly found out that people weren't the least bit confused. In fact, not only were they not confused, but their reaction was also genuinely enthusiastic. It didn't take me long to realize that I was on to something important, and once word about the book spread, I started to receive a surprising number of calls from people asking, "Are you looking for people to interview? Because if you are, I know just the person you need to talk to."

I couldn't believe how many people had interesting stories to tell. It seemed that just about everyone had a neighbor, friend, or relative who was doing something fun and meaningful during semi-retirement. One woman told me about her grandmother, a retired teacher, who was selling an online course she'd written for special needs children; a neighbor spoke about a friend who was working as a travel blogger while enjoying free trips to exotic places; and my client shared stories about her father-in-law, a former advertising executive who was writing a movie script while working part-time as a tour guide for his local historical society.

Others told me about their colleagues who had downshifted from full-time jobs into contract and part-time opportunities that enable them to continue to earn needed income while enjoying a less stressful lifestyle. The stories I heard were as diverse as the individuals who told them.

People who had not yet retired were equally eager to tell me about their future plans: one man shared that he was looking into opportunities with the Peace Corps, another was hoping to sell his paintings, and several other people said they wanted to transition into part-time jobs in their local communities. Interestingly, almost nobody said that they planned to just play golf all day (well, maybe one or two did). One woman in her mid-fifties said of her second-act career plans, "What else am I going to do with myself all day? I plan to live for at least thirty more years, and I need to feel like I have a purpose."

Of course, at the same time that people say they want to work, many baby boomers are struggling with the reality that they will *need* to work. A 2010 Harris poll revealed that a staggering 25 percent of people age forty-six to sixty-four say they have no retirement savings. Even for those who have put money aside for retirement, the triple threat of dwindling pensions, insufficient personal savings, and the uncertainties surrounding Social Security—combined with record levels of personal debt, rising health care costs, and falling real estate values—are forcing many to rethink their retirement plans.

As I write this, my husband and I are rethinking our retirement plans too. We have always worked hard at professional jobs, put the maximum amount allowed into our 401(k)s, lived within our means, never carried credit card debt, and own a house that is thankfully valued at more than we originally paid. According to the experts, all of our efforts should have been more than sufficient to guarantee a comfortable retirement. But even after having done everything "right" and then some, we can't afford to be complacent. Neither of us is eligible for a pension or employer-subsidized health insurance, and the swings in the stock market combined with the meager returns on our investments are giving us cause for concern.

Bottom line? It is clear that we, along with millions of our fellow boomers, will need to find a way to work past the traditional retirement age. Of course, that doesn't mean that we plan to work in the same way, doing the same things, at the same frenetic pace, that we are "forced" to do while employed full-time. In fact, quite the opposite is true. We intend to work—but this time around, we want to be able to do so on our own terms, on our own timetable, and in our own way. This time, we plan to call the shots.

Whether out of necessity, desire, or a combination of the two, it is clear that millions of boomers will soon be looking for ways to reinvent their careers without a traditional 9-to-5 job. We will work during a phase known as "semi-retirement"—the stage that occurs after the big full-time job ends and before full retirement sets in.

I'm assuming that if you picked up this book, you want that too. But is it really possible? Can you find work options that are fun, fulfilling, and flexible—and also give you enough time (and money) for travel, leisure, learning, and other personal interests?

I believe that you can. In fact, I am sure of it. In doing the research for this book, I spoke at length with nearly forty people, most of whom were in their fifties and sixties, who are having the time of their lives working in their second acts. And even though they typically no longer earn what they once did, they are energized, engaged, and connected to their communities; they feel valued, are learning new skills, and know they are making a difference. When asked how long they planned to continue working, the vast majority said they have no intention of slowing down anytime soon; they are simply having too much fun. As Eve Young, a sixty-year-old woman who juggles two part-time jobs as an interfaith minister and acting extra, puts it, "When I'm too old to stand up, then I'll stop."

While it is true that the outlook for the traditional job market continues to appear bleak, I am convinced that the future for boomers who want to pursue flexible and entrepreneurial work options looks very promising indeed. Why? Consider the following:

- **Technology has completely revolutionized how, where, and when we work.** Thanks to wireless networks and mobile technologies, you can now work from just about anywhere: while sitting in your backyard, on a boat, in a coffee shop, or in your mobile home.

- **The options for flexible employment have improved and diversified.** Telecommuting has become increasingly commonplace, and a growing number of companies are offering work-from-home alternatives.

- **The costs of running your own business have decreased dramatically, and the global reach of the Internet has made it possible to sell to anyone, anytime, anywhere.** Gone are the days when you needed a storefront to sell products, a printer to produce a newsletter, or a classroom to teach your lessons. With so many inexpensive and sophisticated tools readily available on the Web, you can now sell products on your website, send out your newsletter electronically, and teach classes online. If you don't want to run your own website, you can sell your handicrafts on sites like Etsy.com, your informational products on Clickbank.com, or your collection of vintage clothing on eBay.com. Going from idea to income can take less than a day and cost less than one hundred dollars!

- **We are fast becoming a nation of freelance workers**, and although that is an arguably problematic trend for many people— especially younger workers—it is an opportunity for boomers who like project work and no longer want to deal with the demands of full-time employment.

- **The Internet provides us unlimited access to information and training twenty-four hours a day.** Thinking about starting a gift basket business? Google the term "gift basket business," and in a matter of seconds you'll find videos, courses, associations, and conferences designed to help you learn how to get this type of business off the ground. Need help after you get your business started? You can post a question to an industry group on LinkedIn or send out a query on Twitter. Interested in finding a seasonal job with the National Park Service? There are job boards where you can easily locate those openings. Looking for training to help you learn how to write grants or start a nonprofit? You can find multiple websites that will teach you all about those skills. I could go on and on, but suffice it to say there is no end to the amount of useful career and business information you'll find online.

Of course, the sheer volume of all this information can lead to information overload. It is hard to know where to begin your research, which sources to trust, and how to figure out what you want to do, especially if you've spent the bulk of your professional life working more or less in one career or industry.

That is why I wrote this book. It will help you sort through the options as you move away from the "big" career and begin to phase into this next stage of your life. This book is divided into two parts. The first highlights more than fifty different models for turning your passions into profits, your interests into income, and your hobbies into cash. The second offers a variety of exercises that will you help you better understand your motivating skills and interests, clarify your lifestyle goals, and help you begin to plan for your next act. After all, it's great to read inspirational stories and learn about new ideas and resources, but at some point you need to turn those dreams into actions that work for *you*. Here is a brief overview of the chapters:

Part One. 50+ Ways to Generate Income in Semi-Retirement

Chapter One: Build Multiple Streams of Expert Income. All of us have special knowledge, experiences, and skills that can be monetized through a variety of "expert" income streams such as consulting, coaching, teaching, training, and speaking. In chapter one, you'll learn about the different models for turning your expertise into multiple streams of income. You'll get to meet a sixty-year-old woman who runs a highly successful coaching business, a lawyer turned mediator, and a former Microsoft executive who teaches marketing to magicians.

Chapter Two: Create an Information Empire. Chapter two explores the different avenues, and new models, for turning your expertise into informational products; it features interviews with a mom who runs a food blog, a woman who makes a healthy five-figure annual income selling digital downloads while enjoying life in Hawaii, and an interview with an expert on "Making Money in Your Jammies."

Chapter Three: Start a Small Service Business. Looking for a home-based business that is easy to start on a shoestring budget? Service businesses can be run from home, operated on a part-time basis, and require minimal start-up expenses—an enticing combination for boomers wanting a lifestyle-friendly income stream. In this chapter, you'll learn about dozens of different types of service businesses, including personal, business support, and pet care options.

Chapter Four: Pursue a Business-in-a-Box Opportunity. Not everyone wants to start a business from scratch. If the thought of being totally on your own makes you uneasy, you may instead want to consider a business-in-a-box opportunity, such as a franchise, direct sales, or licensing arrangement. Although many people have a negative impression of multilevel marketing companies and franchises, I think you'll be pleasantly surprised by what you'll learn about these options in chapter four. People you'll meet in this chapter include a woman who sells clothing as an independent fashion consultant with a direct sales company, a franchisee with a company that supports female entrepreneurs, and a disabled veteran who became a power seller on eBay.

Chapter Five: Trade Your Time for a Paycheck. This chapter explores the different ways you can earn income as a part-time employee, temporary worker, virtual employee, freelancer, or seasonal worker. It includes tips from a woman who runs a flexible jobs board, an interview with the president of an interim executive services firm, and advice from the founder of CoolWorks.com, a job board that features jobs in "cool places."

Chapter Six: Make a Living While Making a Difference. Many boomers are looking for an "encore career," a term that refers to career paths that combine passion, purpose, and income during the second half of life. Chapter six examines five different encore career paths and includes interviews with several inspirational boomers who are using their second-act careers to change the world for the better.

Chapter Seven: Get Paid to Travel. Chapter seven highlights nine different ways that you can get paid to travel (or at least paid enough to offset the costs of your travel), including tour director, tour guide, import-export businesses, temporary innkeeper, working on cruise ships, and ideas for volunteer vacations. But be warned, by the time you get done reading this chapter, you could be infected with a serious case of wanderlust!

Chapter Eight: Ten Reinvention Lessons Learned. In between part one and two, I discuss the ten key reinvention lessons learned from the people profiled in this book. We'll take a look at the factors that helped them be successful and consider ways that you can apply those same strategies to your own reinvention plans.

Part Two. Creating Your Second-Act Career

Chapter Nine: Envision the Life You Want. Building a fulfilling second-act career revolves around both lifestyle and career decisions. The exercises in this chapter will help you to better understand the personal motivators, lifestyle goals, and financial objectives impacting your next act.

Chapter Ten: Look to the Past for Clues to Your Future. Introspection is a key step in the reinvention process. Chapter ten offers guidance on how to collect and organize your personal history into a format that will allow you to more easily complete this task.

Chapter Eleven: Ask, Analyze, and Assess. Although many of you have undoubtedly changed jobs many times, and some of you may have changed careers several times, the descriptor "second-act" refers to making a distinct shift from your prior career path during the second half of life. The exercises in this chapter will help you to better understand your strengths, values and skills so that you can navigate this transition with greater clarity, purpose and ease.

Chapter Twelve: Research the World of Possibilities. Once you know what you love to do, do well, and find meaningful, the next step in this process is to identify real-world opportunities that are a good match for your interests. Chapter twelve overviews the "best-of-the-best" from the world of career research: dozens of resources to help you explore interesting and unusual career possibilities.

Chapter Thirteen: Try It Out! No matter how intriguing a career idea sounds, you'll never know if it is truly a good match until you've had a chance to try it out in the real world. This chapter highlights a variety of low-risk ways to test out potential new directions.

Conclusion: Some Final Tips on Creating Your Second-Act Career. The conclusion offers strategies for ensuring lasting success as you move forward.

As you will soon learn, this book covers a diverse assortment of ideas for creating income on a flexible basis during semi-retirement. Not every idea will appeal to or be a good fit for every reader. But I do think that you will find plenty of surprising and attractive options for building a second-act career, so I encourage you to keep an open mind.

My hope is that this book will help expand your horizons, empower you with knowledge, and leave you feeling inspired, hopeful, and excited about your future. Welcome, in advance, to your second-act career. I think you'll be delighted by what you'll find here.

—Nancy Collamer
mylifestylecareer.com

50+ Ways to Generate Income in Semi-Retirement

One of my favorite childhood memories is of a restaurant called Sweden Towers, which back in the 1960s was known as *the* smorgasbord restaurant on the south shore of Long Island. At the time, the concept of an all-you-can-eat restaurant was relatively new, and I can still remember my mouth watering as I walked around the buffet table surveying all the delectable choices: little Swedish meatballs swimming in gravy, butter cookies with chocolate sprinkles, and wiggly red Jell-O salads garnished with mini marshmallows. I must have asked my parents at least three times, "You mean I can take anything I want as many times as I want?" To which my parents would reply, "Yes, but don't just fill up your plate with spaghetti. Try a few new things for a change."

Reading the first part of this book is a bit like going to Sweden Towers; it offers a smorgasbord of possibilities designed to whet your appetite as you begin to ponder your second-act career. Some of the ideas—like consulting, working a part-time job, or teaching—will be quite familiar to you. Others—like creating your own informational products, training as a mediator, or working as an extra on a movie set—might seem a bit unusual. I've strived to present a well-balanced menu of options, although I must admit that deciding what to include made me feel a bit like that wide-eyed little girl in the restaurant all over again—it was difficult to limit myself! Nonetheless, the opportunities in part one all meet the following six criteria:

1. **Work-life flexibility.** These are work options that can realistically be done on a flexible schedule. You can decide to work them on a part-time or full-time basis, as you prefer. Knowing that many of you hope to be able to travel or work from home during your semi-retirement, I was also careful to include opportunities that can be done on a virtual basis and steered away from brick-and-mortar businesses like restaurants, bakeries, farms, and retail shops that typically require full-time attention (and a large upfront capital investment).

2. **Scalability.** These ideas can work as stand-alone income streams or you can combine several options together to generate multiple income streams (also known as a "portfolio career"). For example, whereas you might be happy teaching just one class a semester as an adjunct professor, another reader might want to teach *and/or* write a book *and/or* create a webinar, *and/or* teach on a cruise ship. Many people start off with one income stream and then slowly add on other profit centers as their time and circumstances allow. You can mix-and-match the options to best meet your lifestyle and income goals.

3. **Range of income potential.** The careers in this book offer a wide range of earning potential. For example, there are bloggers who barely earn a few hundred dollars a year and others who generate a solid five-figure monthly income; temps who earn a few hundred each month and others who get paid the equivalent of a full-time professional salary; direct sales people who are happy making just a few thousand dollars a year and superstars who generate six-figure incomes. When possible, I have included income information with the profiles (current as of the time of this writing), but it's important to remember that, although traditional jobs have somewhat standard salary ranges, the amount you earn as a freelancer or entrepreneur is ultimately determined more by your individual effort, background, credentials, marketing abilities, and personal circumstances than by the restrictions of a specific job category.

4. **Low start-up costs.** The vast majority of the entrepreneurial ideas in this book are service-oriented options that require minimal start-up capital (often as little as a few hundred dollars and generally no more than one thousand).

5. **Limited additional training requirements.** Most of you will need to invest in some form of additional training (workshops, seminars, certificate programs, and the like) as part of your career transition. That said, I intentionally eliminated any options that

would require you to go back to school for an advanced degree. If you want to pursue a bachelor's or an advanced degree, I applaud you, but I assume that most of you, if given the choice, would prefer to not have to invest in yet another expensive and time-consuming college degree.

6. **Age appropriate.** I hesitated to include this because almost any job can be done at any age, and I know of many people who are actually in better shape at age fifty-five than they were at age twenty. Nonetheless, I deliberately chose to avoid jobs that are physically demanding and could prove taxing as you age. Conversely, I favored jobs where age, experience, and maturity are perceived as a competitive advantage.

There are more than fifty different career and business ideas for you to learn about in part one. But you are certainly not limited to these choices; just like an apple can be baked into a pie, crushed into applesauce, or chopped into a cobbler with equally delicious results, each of these career ideas can be sliced, diced, and assembled in hundreds of different ways that satisfy your unique interests, goals, and income needs. As you read through this section, please remember that while the descriptions provided are designed to give you a "taste" of each career, they do not cover all the specifics (licensing requirements, income potential, zoning restrictions, and so on) that you'll need in order to make a truly informed decision. Every career and entrepreneurial option, no matter the focus or industry, comes with its own set of risks, regulations, and rewards; it is up to you to research and fully consider every aspect. I have included information about income potential and licensing requirements when possible, but the specifics change over time, and I encourage you to use the resources provided alongside these descriptions and profiles to help you continue to explore and learn more on your own.

And now, with that understanding in mind, I invite you to pull up a chair, take your seat at the table, and get ready to work up an appetite. It's time to sample the smorgasbord of semi-retirement careers. *Bon appétit!*

CHAPTER ONE

Build Income from Your Expertise

If you have invaluable information, expertise, and life lessons that you want to share with the world and get paid for (and who doesn't?), then this chapter is going to be of great interest to you. Each of you is an expert at something related to your professional experience, hobbies, or personal life. You may be a whiz at technology, a pro at planning events, a scholar on the Civil War, or an expert on the subject of getting into college. Whatever your specialty, it's important to remember that you do not need to be *the* leading expert, practitioner, or guru in your field to make money from your expertise; if you know more than 90 percent of the population knows on any given topic, you can probably find a way to profit from it.

So how can you monetize that expertise?

In this chapter, you'll find a number of different ways to profit from your knowledge capital. You will meet people who have taken bits and pieces of their expertise, added new elements, and blended them all together to create income streams that take advantage of their special talents. Instead of relying on one employer for their livelihood, they generate their income through multiple income options, including coaching, teaching, speaking, and performing. Many of them also supplement their income with the sale of informational products—a subject that we will explore in more depth in the next chapter. But for now, let's kick things off by taking a closer look at consulting, one of the most popular of all semi-retirement careers.

CONSULTANT

If you ask a group of boomers what they plan to do in retirement, you can bet that at least one of them is going to respond with "I'm thinking about doing some consulting." It is no wonder that consulting is often at the top of the semi-retirement careers wish list. Life as a consultant allows you to capitalize on your work experiences, contacts, and expertise, while enjoying the benefits of being your own boss. If you consult on a part-time basis, you'll still have the flexibility to do the things you want to do in retirement. And if, like many new consultants, you start your business by consulting to your former employer, it can prove to be a nice way to remain connected to your colleagues without the commitment of a full-time job.

What types of consulting can you do? Consultants advise companies, organizations, and entrepreneurs on a multitude of issues, including:

- **Management issues.** Management consultants advise companies on "big picture" topics like strategic planning, operations, and technology. These consulting assignments tend to be high-visibility, high-risk, and high-reward projects that are best for people willing to work long hours in sometimes stressful environments.

- **Industry-specific issues.** Companies hire consultants who have strong industry expertise to work on issues that cannot be adequately addressed by their own internal employees. For example, a former military officer might be asked to consult on security matters, or an insurance executive might be retained to consult on risk management policies.

- **Business processes.** Some consultants specialize in advising companies and organizations on better ways to handle specific tasks like fund-raising, social media outreach, or managing public relations campaigns. Consultants are also brought in to provide counsel in response to newly enacted regulations and laws.

- **Business development.** Companies of all sizes, from start-ups to large corporations, hire consultants who can help them find more clients, make more sales, and develop new sources of revenue.

- **Business advisory and forecasting services.** In every industry there are "gurus" who get paid handsomely to speak, consult, and write about the trends and technologies that impact the future direction and profitability of the industry.

Before you start work as a consultant, you will want to be very clear about your unique value proposition: what it is you bring to the table and how it will benefit your clients. Although many consultants launch their practices with a wide-ranging menu of services, most quickly discover that it is easier to offer a well-defined niche expertise than to try to be all things to all people. Like any entrepreneurial endeavor, consulting has its challenges. The unpredictable cash flow, feelings of isolation, and lack of support systems can make this a difficult choice if you are accustomed to the predictability and support of corporate life. In general, consultants to large companies earn the highest fees, but in exchange they are expected to work long hours and travel wherever and whenever the client needs them. As a result, many semi-retired people prefer to consult to smaller organizations, entrepreneurs, and nonprofits because they tend to offer a more lifestyle-friendly consulting alternative.

Because consulting is such a popular career choice, there is no shortage of resources available to help you learn about this option:

- Start your research by asking other people who are working as consultants in your field for their advice on best practices within your industry. If you don't personally know of anyone, you can always find consultants by asking colleagues for referrals or by doing a Google search using the name of your industry and the word "consultant" as search terms.

- Investigate the consulting workshops and programs offered through your local community colleges and continuing education programs. Check the offerings of SCORE (previously known as the Service Corps of Retired Executives), a nonprofit association with hundreds of local offices offering free business mentoring and low-cost workshops (www.score.org), or the US Small Business Administration (www.sba.gov) for listings of helpful workshops, webinars, and consulting services—many of which are provided free or for a low cost.

- Check with your professional industry association to learn about their training offerings for consultants.

Recommended reading: *Million Dollar Consulting: The Professional's Guide to Building Your Platform* by Alan Weiss (McGraw-Hill, 2010). Weiss is widely regarded as *the* authority on how to succeed as an independent management consultant and has authored many books on this subject. Although his books are geared toward people who want to be full-time consultants, his advice can easily be adapted to meet the needs of part-time consultants as well.

COACH

At a time when people increasingly operate as "lone cowboys" in both their personal and professional lives, it is no surprise that the popularity of working with a coach—and *as* a coach—is on the rise. As opposed to consultants who get paid primarily to give advice, coaches focus on both the mechanics and the mind-set of solving problems, helping their clients to overcome self-defeating behaviors and achieve greater success. There are coaches for just about every type of life situation imaginable including life, career, executive, and financial issues. And within those broader coaching categories there are subspecialties: executive coaches who coach only Hispanic women, life coaches who cater to divorced women, and financial coaches who specialize in retirement planning. You name it and there is a coach for it—and no matter what your area of expertise, it is possible to find a way to build a coaching service around it.

Coaching is a relatively new profession, and as such, the standards for licensing and credentialing are still being formulated. For the time being, virtually anyone can hang out a shingle and declare that she or he is a coach. The low barriers to becoming a coach, along with the misconception that anyone can earn a high hourly rate for "just talking with people on the phone," means that there are a lot of people who aspire to be coaches—but not everyone succeeds. Executive coach Douglas Campbell III warns that you need to be prepared to market your services very effectively in order to distinguish yourself from the crowd. "There are a lot of wannabe coaches out there," says Doug. "But I think less than 30 percent of the coaches are actually making a living from it."

One of the great appeals of coaching as a semi-retirement career is the lifestyle it allows: you can set your own hours, work from anywhere, and once you've established a strong following it is possible to earn an impressive income. Most coaches work with clients by telephone, although executive coaches often meet with their clients in person. Coaching rates range from $75 per hour for novice life coaches up to $1,000 per hour for top executive, small business, and celebrity coaches. However, even top coaches find that it can be hard to make a living from coaching sessions alone, so many coaches supplement their income with the sale of training programs, books, seminars, and other offerings that complement their coaching services. Established coaches also earn income by teaching and coaching other coaches in the "business of the business."

There are hundreds of training programs for aspiring coaches: from degree and certificate programs at major universities, to full-year programs run by coaching institutes, to online niche coaching programs developed by enterprising entrepreneurs. The quality and credibility of these programs vary widely, and different programs focus on different specialty areas, so do take the time to find a program that meets your specific goals and interests. Consult with other coaches to get their recommendations on the best programs for your unique needs.

Here are some resources for further exploration:

- **International Coaching Federation (ICF) (www.coachfederation .org).** The world's leading coaching organization, ICF provides credentialing, certification programs, conferences, and research for the coaching profession. ICF members include life coaches, executive coaches, career coaches, and business coaches. The ICF has active local chapters around the globe.

- **Coaches Training Institute (CTI) (www.thecoaches.com).** The world's oldest and largest in-person coach training organization, CTI offers a number of highly regarded training programs for both new and experienced coaches. The founders of CTI wrote an excellent book about coaching, *Co-Active Coaching: Changing Business, Transforming Lives* (Nicholas Brealey Publishing, 2011), that is considered a classic on coaching techniques.

- **Peterson's (www.petersons.com).** This site lists universities and colleges that offer coaching programs and classes.

THREE TIPS FROM THE ENTREPRENEURIAL EXPERT

**"Don't forget to have fun: part of the reason you
start your own business is to enjoy life."**
—DOUGLASS CAMPBELL III, CEO, executive coach, and managing
director of the Success Coach (www.thesuccesscoach.com)

Doug Campbell knows what it takes to run a successful business. An executive coach since 1996, Doug was the chief marketing officer of a $200-million-dollar division of a Fortune 100
firm, taught MBA programs for the Darden School at the University of Virginia, and has started five businesses. Here are his tips
on how to be a successful entrepreneur:

1. **Surround yourself with good advisers and mentors.** There
   is tremendous value to be gained from actively seeking the
   advice of mentors as you build and grow your business.
   If you don't feel comfortable reaching out and asking for
   feedback on your own, Doug suggests that you consider
   participating in a mastermind group. Several times a year he
   invites a selected group of entrepreneurs to participate in his
   High-Talent Creatives Group, a brainstorming event where
   group members bounce around ideas, share suggestions,
   and learn from each other's experiences. One business is
   chosen to be the focus of the meeting (past participants
   have included the founders of Sobe beverage company and
   Edgar Online), but everyone is given time to speak, network,
   and benefit from the collective wisdom of the group.

2. **Know your risk profile.** There are different levels of risk
   associated with different types of businesses. The level of
   risk you are willing to assume will affect the level of comfort and confidence you are able to bring to your business,
   so choose a business that meshes well with your personal
   tolerance for risk and financial uncertainty.

{continued}

3. **Stop worrying that someone will steal your idea.** Yes, there is a risk that someone will steal your idea, but the way you develop and refine ideas is by soliciting input from other people. "Let's be honest," says Doug. "If you see a need for something, chances are good that at least eight to ten other people around the country have had the same idea." Worry less about somebody stealing the idea; focus more on getting suggestions from other people that will make your idea better and stronger.

TEACHER/TRAINER

Are you a natural teacher? Do you enjoy explaining concepts, theories, and the mechanics of how to do things? Would you like to share the wealth of experiences you've accumulated with others and pass on your knowledge to future generations?

If the prospect of empowering people with the skills, resources, and expertise needed for success in both their personal and professional lives excites you, then you might want to consider sharing your expertise either as a classroom teacher or a "how-to" trainer who instructs via webinars, workshops, or seminars. For people who are outgoing and enjoy an audience, teaching can be a great way to earn an income. Here are some interesting options to consider:

- **Adjunct professor.** Adjunct-level professors are hired on a contractual, nontenured basis to teach at universities, community colleges, vocational schools, and colleges. Some institutions require that their adjuncts meet the same degree requirements as their full-time faculty (meaning you may need a doctorate degree to be hired), whereas at other schools a bachelor's or master's degree is sufficient. Prior teaching experience is always advantageous, but the combination of an advanced degree plus work experience is often sufficient to make you an attractive teaching candidate, especially if you want to teach at a community college or smaller school. Adjuncts don't earn a lot (typically anywhere from a few hundred to a few thousand per course), but adding the word "professor" to your resume or bio can be a great way to enhance your reputation, reach, and marketability.

- **Online instructor.** The world of online education is rapidly gaining traction, credibility, and prestige. Although brick-and-mortar universities tend to use their in-house faculty for online assignments, online institutions hire outside applicants who offer strong subject-related work experience. A master's degree can make you more marketable, but schools will consider applicants who hold a bachelor's degree along with relevant work experience. To find an online teaching position, apply directly to the online institution, or search on one of the many online job boards—for example, Simplyhired.com, Indeed.com, or the jobs listed on the Chronicle of Higher Education site (chronicle.com), using keywords such as "online teacher" or "virtual instructor."

- **Corporate trainer.** Few companies still maintain in-house training departments, and as a result, many have increased their use of outside vendors to train their employees on topics ranging from sales to business etiquette to leadership. To learn more about these opportunities, and to find vendors who might be interested in contracting with you as a freelance trainer, consult the website of the American Society for Training and Development (www.astd.org).

- **Adult education instructor.** Continuing education programs are always in need of new programs, workshops, and classes to fill their catalogs. Although most programs will pay only a small stipend for your services, teaching in one of these programs is an easy and cost-effective way to market and advertise your services. In addition to teaching opportunities at local community colleges, vocational programs, or town continuing education programs, you can teach at privately run adult education programs such as the Learning Annex (www.learningannex.com) or the Gotham Writers' Workshop (www.writingclasses.com).

- **Online trainer.** Thousands of entrepreneurs are generating significant income by creating their own brand of online training programs, formatted as videos, webinars, and multisession "universities." Although many online courses focus on teaching business development and internet marketing, the possibilities for packaging your expertise into your own program to deliver a virtual learning experience are limited only by your imagination. And once you develop a course, you can sell it in multiple formats (downloadable manual, video, podcast, and so on) for as long as the information remains relevant and timely. You can learn more about this option in the next chapter.

- **School owner-director.** As a child, I attended a ballet school taught by one of the neighborhood moms in the attic of her home. It was a simple studio that catered to the needs of the local tutu-lovers while providing a steady income stream for my neighbor while she stayed home to raise her children. This spirit of home-grown entrepreneurship is still alive and well, in the form of home-based cooking schools, language programs for toddlers, and acting classes. Of course, before opening any school in your home, be sure to check with your town and state government for applicable zoning and licensing requirements, especially since your neighbors might protest if your business increases traffic in the neighborhood.

- **One-to-one tutor.** The demand for tutors is always strong, especially for people who can help children improve their grades, study habits, and SAT scores (tutors in affluent neighborhoods can command upward of $150 per hour for their services). If you'd prefer working with adults, consider offering your expertise as a computer and technology tutor. Although most tutors run their own businesses, you can opt to work for one of the big tutoring services, such as Kaplan or Kumon, if you don't want to go it alone.

- **Private teacher.** Would you like to teach people on a one-to-one basis or in a small group setting? The opportunities to profit as a private instructor are limited only by your imagination—people will gladly pay for personalized instruction in any number of interest areas, including yoga, painting, video-editing, and photography.

To learn more about teaching jobs and the training field, consult:

- **Chronicle of Higher Education (chronicle.com).** An online resource for jobs and information related to colleges and universities.

- **American Society for Training and Development (www.astd.org).** The professional organization for people involved in corporate and business-related training and development. Their website is an excellent resource for people interested in all aspects of the training world.

- **HigherEdJobs (www.higheredjobs.com).** Lists openings in academia.

TEACH THE BUSINESS OF THE BUSINESS

Have you ever built a business, turned a business around, or significantly improved the profitability of a business? Do you have strong expertise in marketing or business development? Are you knowledgeable about a specific business process, such as how to get a nonfiction book published, write a press release, design a website, or create a YouTube video? If so, you may be able profit handsomely (very handsomely!) from teaching other entrepreneurs what you know.

We are fast becoming a nation of independent entrepreneurs; according to the Kauffman Index of Entrepreneurial Activity, a leading indicator of new business creation, the share of new fifty-five- to sixty-four-year-old entrepreneurs increased from 14.3 percent in 1996 to 20.9 percent in 2011. This entrepreneurial trend is feeding a growing demand for people who can teach the "business of the business"—that is, all of the business skills needed to start, run, grow, and manage a profitable business.

This is an idea with tremendous income and growth potential. Although most entrepreneurs are great at their core business—they are wonderful photographers, talented jewelers, skilled coaches—they often lack the business skills and knowledge needed to turn their talents into a sustainable business. And even successful business people are not equally skilled at all aspects of running their business; they may be great at cold-calling, but lousy at copywriting; skilled at promotions, but weak at closing the sale; savvy at networking in person, but clueless when it comes to building relationships online. Sadly, no matter how good people are at their craft, if they don't know how to find clients and make the sale, they will eventually go out of business.

Needless to say, the mere threat of going out of business causes entrepreneurs a lot of sleepless nights, so they are more than willing to invest in learning proven techniques for avoiding this fate. Here are a few examples from my own entrepreneurial journey to demonstrate how you might be able to profit from teaching the business of the business:

- **Marketing and publicity.** Most people don't know how to write a press release, get publicity, or handle the publicity once they get it. I sure didn't when I was new to business, but I learned from Marcia Yudkin, who runs a business that teaches people the how-to of business writing and marketing. She sells a wide range of products and services, including books, courses, informational products, and consulting services that teach people how to create compelling content, attract publicity, and better market their services.

- **Business development.** There is no shortage of people eager to teach the basics of business development to new entrepreneurs. In the early stages of my business, I read a very helpful book by

C. J. Hayden called *Get Clients Now!* (Amacom, 2007), which helped me understand the principles and practices associated with building up a private practice. From there, I went on to take other courses to learn about different business development topics including pricing, marketing, and branding.

- **Publishing.** When I first thought about writing a book, I didn't have a clue as to how to find an agent or how to write a book proposal. I learned by reading several helpful books and by attending a few seminars (some free and some for a fee) that helped me better understand the book publishing business. There are people teaching every aspect of the publishing process, including how to run a book blog tour, how to write a book in a month (I probably should have signed up for that one!), and how to make money speaking about your book.

- **Technology.** Technology is constantly changing, and because of this, entrepreneurs have an ongoing need for people who can help them manage their technology issues. I have paid for classes on blogging, website design, and social media networking, and I am certain that I will invest in many more technology classes in the years ahead.

There are infinite ways you might be able to use your skills, industry knowledge, or technical expertise to help other entrepreneurs succeed. But if you do decide to "teach the business of the business," you may find it beneficial to tailor your offerings for a specific industry. For example, within my own industry there are people who specialize in teaching marketing to career coaches. This can be a particularly effective strategy for people who have an established track record of success working in their industry; their credibility tends to be far stronger than that of industry outsiders who sound good in theory but lack the practical experience to back up their theoretical expertise. To illustrate this point, let me pull a rabbit out of my hat and introduce you to Jack Turk of Redmond, Washington, who specializes in a very unique niche— teaching marketing to magicians.

Poof! From Microsoft to a Magical Marketer

"I'm a big multiple streams of income guy, and in this economy, that is not a bad thing."

—Jack Turk, marketer and magician

On the day that Jack Turk turned fifty, he walked into his boss's office, sat down, and announced that he was quitting his job. After a fifteen-year career with Microsoft as a writer, program manager, and game designer, Jack didn't quit to ride off into the sunset—he chose to walk away from his six-figure income to pursue his lifelong passion for the magic business.

Jack first discovered the joy of magic when he was just five years old, and ever since, magic has played an important role in his life. Even when he was employed full-time, he kept up a side business as a magician, performing at family, civic, and corporate events whenever his schedule allowed. While working at his corporate job, Jack learned how to perfect his writing and marketing skills—and those skills enabled him to easily market and advertise his magic shows.

The more adept Jack became at his own marketing, the more he began to notice that his peers in the magic world seemed to struggle with that part of their business. They were skilled magicians, but they had difficulty getting enough work to support their passion. It was painful for Jack to watch. "The magic business is like every other business," says Jack. "Everyone is into what they do, and they think because they are really good at it, then the word will get out and then they will get really busy. But that is not the case. You've got to market yourself."

Jack knew that with his strong writing skills, business background, and firsthand experience as a magician, he could make money by teaching the "business of the business" to other magicians. But rather than starting his own business from scratch, he bought an established site that was run by a man named Dave Dee, who at the time was considered the "magician's marketing guru." Jack had studied with Dave and knew his materials were very helpful. Jack and Dave worked together for a year while they transitioned ownership of the site, and then Jack went from paying the guru all the money to being known as the guru himself.

Today on his website, www.magicmarketingcenter.com, Jack sells a variety of different products and services, ranging from free downloadable reports to live training events that cost thousands of dollars. His offerings include products with titles like "Success Strategies for the Restaurant Magician," "How to Create, Market, and Present Motivational School Assembly Programs for Big Profits," and "How to Make $25,000 Doing Birthday Parties Part-Time." His products and trainings are designed to alleviate the money fears that keep magicians awake at night: fears that revolve around not having enough business and not knowing what to do or say to attract more business. In addition to running his e-commerce site, Jack continues to earn income as a performing magician, working between two to three hundred events per year, the majority of which are birthday parties. And as if that wasn't enough to keep him busy, he also helps to organize technology conferences and takes on a limited number of freelance writing projects.

When asked what advice he has for others who want to build an expert income stream around their passion, Jack suggested the following.

Jack's Top Three Tips for Creating a Successful Business-to-Business Service

1. **Be an active contributor on key online sites**. Every group, every "band of brothers and sisters" has an online meeting place. Identify the popular forums in your niche and post helpful suggestions to these forums on a regular basis. People will learn to trust your recommendations, which will help them be more comfortable purchasing your products and services down the road.

2. **Know your income goals**. As an entrepreneur, it's easy to get diverted by all types of non-revenue-producing activities. Have a target for what you need to earn, and then ask yourself each day, "Am I focused on a task that supports that goal?"

3. **Get out of the house**. The notion that you can do all of your networking online is a fallacy—you have to get out and meet people. Most of Jack's income comes from people whom he has met in person, and over time they have developed strong friendships, co-branded events, and business alliances.

To learn more about how to teach the business of the business, look into the many online courses designed to teach entrepreneurs about how to create curriculum and develop classes, webinars, and training programs:

- Jen Louden and Michele Christensen have an online program called TeachNow (www.theteacherspath.com) for people who want to learn how to teach and put together their own courses.

- Pam Slim of Escape from Cubicle Nation offers an online training course called "Power Teaching" through her website at www .escapefromcubiclenation.com/power-teaching.

SPEAKER

Many people fear public speaking. But even if the idea of being a public speaker scares the heck out of you, it may still be worthwhile to consider speaking as part of your income strategy. Why? Done well, speaking is the single most effective way to market your services and sell your products. People want to buy from vendors whom they know, like, and trust, and speaking gives you an opportunity to establish a personal, lively, and lasting connection with your potential customer base. And although speaking can be an intimidating prospect for certain personalities, it's helpful to remember that with a little bit of practice, speaking skills can be learned and nerves can be conquered.

If you've got industry expertise, an inspirational message, a keen sense of humor, or a unique perspective, trust that somebody, somewhere, is going to want to hear what you have to say. Speakers work in a variety of settings and presentation formats. Inexperienced speakers can try out their speaking skills at local community groups like the Lions Club, schools, churches, and synagogues. Of course, as a newbie speaker, it's unlikely that you will be paid much, if anything, for these local talks. But even if you don't earn more than a free dinner, you can leverage your talks as a marketing tool that leads to other speaking invitations. Over time, as you develop your reputation as a speaker, it will be much easier to ask to be paid for your talks.

Who will hire you to speak? You'd be surprised. There are more groups out there than you could ever imagine. Conferences, associations, corporations, colleges, the military, and even nonprofit organizations hire speakers to address a wide variety of topics. Although there is no one single topic that is *the* golden ticket to speaking success, certain types of speakers definitely command higher fees than others: celebrities, professionals with strong technical expertise, people who can teach a "proven formula" for increasing sales or building a business, leadership experts, and motivational speakers are all in demand.

There are several different ways to generate revenues from your speaking engagements. First and most obvious is to get paid a speaker's fee, which could range from a few hundred dollars for a small group presentation to tens of thousands of dollars for prime-time keynote speeches. The exact amount you'll earn will depend on a variety of factors, but in general you'll command the highest fees from corporations and larger associations. In addition to speaking fees, you can earn income from "back of the room" sales of books, videos, and other informational products. Another possibility is to host your own speaking gigs—private presentations, workshops, and seminars—a potentially lucrative option because you get to pocket all the profits after expenses. Most speakers also generate indirect profits from their talks by using them as a platform to market their products and services. According to a survey conducted by the National Speakers Association (NSA) in 2007, the majority of professional speakers supplement their speaking income with higher-end offerings like consulting, coaching, and training services.

Of course, the rewards of life as a speaker extend far beyond just the financial gains. The opportunity to speak in different places can be a very attractive perk for people who love to travel. For outgoing personalities who relish the thrill of a interacting with a live audience, speaking provides a fun way to make a living, much more so than the more solitary existence of being a writer. And for many speakers, particularly those who have a strong message to share, the opportunity to inspire, empower, and change people's lives for the better often proves to be the greatest reward of all.

ADVICE FROM THE SPEAKING EXPERT

"I've always believed that work can be rewarding and fun, but being a speaker has confirmed it for me."
—GILDA BONANNO, speaker, trainer, coach

Gilda Bonanno of Stamford, CT, runs her own public speaking coaching and training business and travels around the globe to places as diverse as China, Brazil, and Rome: she presents keynotes, delivers corporate training programs, and coaches individuals to be more effective public speakers. Her speaking topics range from leadership development to improvisational techniques to presentation skills. She started the business in 1996 following a career as a project manager for a pharmaceutical company and in just seven short years, she has gone from being a novice speaker to president of the Connecticut Speakers Association, past president of the Southern Connecticut Chapter of the American Society of Training and Development, and a contributing author to the National Speakers Association's flagship book *Paid to Speak: Best Practices for Building a Successful Speaking Business* (Greenleaf Book Group Press, 2011). I asked Gilda, a former client of mine, to share her tips for people who want to break into the speaking profession, and she graciously agreed.

What is the best way to get started in the speaking profession?

G.B: Start by speaking about what you know. When you focus on an area where you know the issues and people, you avoid positioning yourself as a newbie speaker and instead establish yourself as an expert who also happens to speak.

This seems like a profession where experience and age can be used to your advantage. Do you agree?

G.B: I do! People who have proven experience in the trenches bring tremendous credibility to the table. Your audience knows that you "get it." Use your old career and established network as a bridge to new opportunities. Build on your experiences and connections and then branch out from there.

What advice do you have for people who want to polish their speaking skills?

G.B: The first goal is to speak as much as possible, for free if you need to. Getting experience in front of groups will allow you to refine your message and your skills. Every town has organizations and associations in need of speakers. Hone your skills by joining Toastmasters, videotaping yourself, and if needed, consider hiring a speaking coach.

How did you learn about the business side of speaking and training?

G.B: I joined my local chapters of the National Speakers Association and American Society for Training & Development to learn more about the business side of speaking. I also asked other speakers that I respected for their suggestions on the best resources for educating myself about the business. You need to be careful about what you buy; there is a lot of information out there that is gimmicky and only designed to make the seller money. One of my favorite books on the business of speaking is *Million Dollar Speaking* by Alan Weiss.

You have been very active in your professional associations. Do you recommend that to others?

G.B: The opportunity to volunteer with professional associations is important, and it's a great way to make connections. But it's also important not to confuse going to meetings and serving on the board as [equivalent to] getting out there and being a speaker. Don't allow yourself to be pulled into that trap.

What are some of the challenges of being a speaker?

G.B: The travel can be tough, so be mindful of your lifestyle objectives when making your choices. Almost all of the speakers I know depend upon multiple streams of income (monthly coaching programs, seminars, membership sites, audio and video products, and so on). It enables you to weather the economic storms and generate income without the need to travel all the time.

A final note: Regardless of whether or not you want to pursue the speaking option, take seven minutes and watch Gilda's inspirational video, "28,000 Days," on her website (www.gildabonanno .com)—it will encourage you to stay focused and on task as you go through your own reinvention process.

To learn more about the speaking industry:

- American Society for Training & Development (www.astd.org)
- National Speakers Association (www.nsaspeaker.org)
- Toastmasters International (www.toastmasters.org)
- Speaker Net News (www.speakernetnews.com)

CREATE EVENTS AND HAPPENINGS FOR YOUR "TRIBE"

People are social beings, and in a world that is increasingly connected by high-tech electronics, the need for in-person, high-touch interaction is stronger than ever. Many people want opportunities to get together, laugh, and enjoy face-to-face conversations. As you consider ways to earn money as an expert in your field, think about how you might be able to create special events, groups, and gatherings for your community. If you let your imagination go wild, you'll find that the opportunities to connect your community are almost endless. For example, you could:

- Sponsor a conference, expo, or lecture series.
  Revenue potential: vendor fees, admission fees, and sponsorships

- Organize a job fair, crafts fair, or gift expo.
  Revenue potential: vendor fees, sponsorships, and commissions from sales

- Create a support group that enables people who share a common need (for example, job seekers, entrepreneurs, caregivers) to come together to exchange resources, share leads, compare strategies, and enjoy a safe haven of like-minded peers.
  Revenue potential: membership fees, event fees, and sponsorship fees paid by affiliated service providers

- Organize a special trip or outing (or series of trips).
  Revenue potential: event fees and referral fees from participating merchants or vendors

- Plan a monthly social or learning event series.
  Revenue potential: event fees and referral fees from participating merchants or vendors

- Build an "online mall" where your tribe can easily sell their products and services.

    Revenue potential: listing fees, membership fees, and advertising revenues

- Compile essays and articles from your peers into a book.

    Revenue potential: income from sales of the book and partnership opportunities

- Start an association.

    Revenue potential: membership fees, product sales, advertising revenues, and the opportunity to earn revenues from add-on services like training programs, books, and special events

Of course, not everyone is well suited to lead a community or host group events. But for the right personality, this can be a really fun way to earn a living. Read on to learn how one business coach is generating multiple streams of income by continually innovating new events and services for her community.

From Artist to "Soul" Proprietor

"Network, network, network: sometimes you don't know where it will lead, but everything I have achieved in my business has come from a business relationship."
—Jane Pollak, author of *Soul Proprietor*

Hard as it may be to believe, Jane Pollak used to earn her living painting eggs. Of course, these were no ordinary kitchen eggs; they were intricately painted Ukrainian Easter eggs that Jane made into jewelry and collectible pieces. They were so unique that she was even asked to make a special egg for the Easter egg roll at the White House, a contribution that is now housed in the Smithsonian Institution. Jane went on to write a book about her eggs, and her business was featured on NBC's *Today* show.

But after spending thirty years being known as "the egg lady," Jane decided she was ready for a change. As she notes in her second book,

Soul Proprietor: 101 Lessons from a Lifestyle Entrepreneur (Roberts Press, 2010), "I felt that artistically I had already said everything in eggs that I needed to say." In a seeming wink from the universe, her decision to switch gears from being an artist to coaching artists was cemented when the week she was supposed to be on *The Martha Stewart Show* turned out to be the same week that Martha went off to jail.

By the time she made the final decision to pack up her paintbrushes, clean out her studio, and shift her focus to coaching other entrepreneurs, Jane was carefully positioned for success. She had always invested heavily in her entrepreneurial education: making it a habit to listen to motivational tapes, attend seminars, and read everything she could about entrepreneurship. She served a term as president of the Entrepreneurial Woman's Network of Westport, Connecticut, a group dedicated to educating, supporting, and inspiring female entrepreneurs. As she gained confidence in her entrepreneurial expertise, Jane began to build up her speaking career: delivering motivational speeches focused on the message that if she could make a living out of painting eggs, surely others could earn their living pursuing a passion too.

Jane organized a group of local artists into the Artsy Girls, an informal networking group that continues to meet on a quarterly basis to socialize, talk about projects, and support one another in their professional and artistic endeavors. When several members of the Artsy Girls expressed interest in receiving more formal entrepreneurial education, Jane responded by creating Jane Pollak's Arts Forum, a monthly coaching group composed of ten artists eager to take their businesses to the next level. The Arts Forum proved so successful that Jane began offering group coaching to people outside her original network of artists. As she got more involved with the coaching arm of her business, Jane decided to invest in formal coach training with the Coaches Training Institute, and she earned her designation as a Certified Professional Co-Active Coach (CPCC). In addition to coaching individuals on a one-to-one basis, she offered multiday coaching retreats and she began to tour the country as a speaker, sharing her entrepreneurial lessons with both new and seasoned business owners.

Her business did extremely well until the financial downturn of 2008. But when tough times hit, Jane responded to the business challenges by revamping her offerings to be more in sync with the new economic climate. She created the Remarkable Women's networking evenings: a by-invitation-only event restricted to thirty women. (Jane often runs the events in the studios and stores of other entrepreneurs who offer their space in exchange for the free publicity and exposure.) "The energy in the room is always amazing," says Jane, noting that the events are characterized by purposeful networking and a generous spirit of sharing mixed with a large dose of fun. More recently, Jane added a webinar series to her mix of services, a lower-priced offering that has prompted long-time fans to finally become paying clients. Jane says, "I have people who I met six years ago who are now able to afford me. It's amazing how they come out of the woodwork when you are able to offer something that fits their needs."

In a field in which many coaches struggle to make a living, and at an age when most people plan to slow down, Jane, age sixty-four, is proud to say, "I earn six figures starting with the number one, working three days a week." As a new grandmother, that level of flexibility is especially precious to her—when her granddaughter Chloe was born, Jane happily promised her daughter that she would reserve one day a week for babysitting duties. But even while making more time for her personal life, she is determined to continue to "live life big," and her goals for the business remain as ambitious as ever. "My ultimate vision is to address thirty thousand business owners at Madison Square Garden," says Jane. "I don't know what the forum will be, but I see myself from the stage talking to them. Somehow that will happen."

Jane's Top Three Tips for Entrepreneurial Success

1. **Don't go it alone.** Join a mastermind group, team up with an accountability buddy, hire a coach, and make it a point to always invest in education. Jane proudly admits to using all of these support systems as part of her ongoing career development. "I work very hard on myself all the time," she says. And, of course, make it a habit to network. Sometimes your networking won't yield immediate results, but over time your efforts will be handsomely rewarded.

2. **Take a measuring stick to your passion.** At this point in your life, you should choose to do work that you love. What they say is true—when you love what you do, what you do is not work.

3. **Be persistent.** Don't quit before the miracle. If you stay in the game, you're going to win.

RECRUITER

Is your Rolodex bulging with business cards gathered from years of networking and business meetings? If so, you may be able to leverage those connections by working as a recruiter. This is a career option for which age can definitely play in your favor. As a veteran member of your industry, it is likely that you not only know a lot of people but also possess a real understanding of the technical expertise, personal characteristics, and skills needed to be a top performer in your field. That combination of networking connections and industry insights could help you be a very successful industry recruiter. There are several different ways you could potentially work as a recruiter:

- **Get hired by an executive search firm.** Executive search professionals help companies fill top-level management jobs and assist them throughout the hiring process—sourcing prospects, coaching candidates on interview skills, and running background checks. Successful recruiters tend to be good salespeople; they know how to bring parties together, negotiate through objections, and close deals. Executive search is the most highly compensated type of recruiting (fees can average up to 25 percent or more of a first-year salary). Be forewarned, however, that full-time recruiters with large firms tend to work long hours, including evening and weekends, so if you need flexibility, negotiate for a part-time role or work for a boutique recruitment agency instead.

- **Create your own niche recruitment agency.** You can hang out your shingle as an independent recruiter who specializes in filling jobs within a specific industry niche. For example, while research-ing this book, I learned of a man who had worked as a yacht club manager for many years and was starting a recruiting service that will specialize in sourcing yacht club staff. It is also possible to work as a contract researcher who does the behind-the-scenes research that helps agencies locate suitable candidates for their searches.

- **Work as a temporary recruiter.** Contract recruiters are used by companies to help staff-up for specific hiring needs, such as when a business is opening a new store or needs extra help for the holidays. You can find these opportunities advertised on the major job boards or by directly contacting temporary employ-ment agencies.

To learn more, look into the Association of Executive Search Con-sultants (AESC; www.aesc.org), the professional body for the executive search industry. They offer a number of useful resources and training programs for search professionals.

MEDIATOR

We live in a litigious society. But going to court is an expensive and pain-ful process that often leaves everyone involved dissatisfied. In contrast, the mediation process allows people to come up with a solution that both parties find acceptable, without having to incur the astronomical fees and aggravation associated with filing a lawsuit. That is why more people are hiring mediators as an alternative for settling workplace dis-putes, divorces, and other types of contentious disagreements.

It might surprise you to learn that all that is required to become a mediator in the United States is to complete a forty-hour basic mediation training class. Of course, what is officially required and what is needed to launch a successful practice are two different matters; experienced mediators warn that completing the basic class is not nearly enough to prepare you to be an effective practitioner. If you want to be taken seriously, before you accept any paying clients you should plan to invest in further education by taking additional seminars, working at volunteer assignments, and interning—in other words, learning by doing.

There are many different ways to work as a mediator. Two of the more popular specializations are divorce and parent-child mediation, but mediators also help to resolve disputes in the workplace, religious institutions, schools, nursing homes, hospitals, and neighborhoods. If you think about your own industry, or life experience, you could probably come up with some interesting ways to specialize in dispute resolution in the field you know well. After all, you have far greater familiarity with the potential disputes common to your area of expertise than the average person, and that experience could make you a very effective mediator. To better understand how this works in practice, read on to learn how one enterprising woman from Armonk, New York, has built up a successful mediation practice resolving disputes in a most unusual specialty.

From Litigator to Mediator: A Heartwarming "Tail"

"Encouraging conversation often alleviates the need for litigation."
—Debra Hamilton, Esq., owner of Hamilton Law
    and Mediation, PLLC

When you hear the term "pet business," you likely think about options like dog walker, groomer, or vet. But Debra Hamilton, age fifty-four, owner of Hamilton Law and Mediation, a firm that specializes in resolving animal disputes, has one of the most unique pet-oriented businesses you'll ever encounter. A lawyer by training, Debra worked as a litigator before taking time off to stay home with her children. But after her son entered first grade, Debra decided it was time to dust off her legal skills and return to paid employment. Reluctant to return to the stresses of life as a litigator, Debra decided instead to train as a mediator, and in 2010 she opened her mediation practice.

Why did she choose to specialize in animal-related disputes? As a lifelong dog lover and breeder of championship dogs, Debra had long been passionate about helping animals. But as a practicing lawyer, she discovered that the courts are required to treat animals like property, and as a result, the courts rarely resolve animal disputes in a way that anyone finds effective. Debra's experience with the court system convinced her that mediation is much better than litigation for resolving animal-related problems. As she notes on her website, "Treating an animal as a mere object when resolving a dispute in a confrontational litigious setting creates unnecessary contention and divisiveness." Using mediation as an alternative to litigation, Debra is able to help her clients, and their four-legged friends, find a mutually satisfactory resolution to their conflicts.

Debra helps to mediate all types of animal-related conflicts: from family-related pet issues (for example, who gets to keep the dog when a couple divorces), to conflicts involving animal trainers and veterinarians, to animal-related arguments that erupt between owners, breeders, and handlers. Using her trademark kind and gentle style, Debra guides the two feuding parties to an agreement that is a win-win for all involved. "Mediators create a venue where people can solve their own problems," says Debra. "I provide an environment where they can say what they have to say—with passion and with anger and with whatever they need to do to get the conversation to the next level."

Debra charges $500 an hour for her services (with a two-hour minimum), and most cases take about six hours to resolve. Both parties involved in the mediation assume equal responsibility for her fee, and payment is required regardless of whether or not an agreement is reached. If the conflict cannot be resolved, the parties can opt to proceed to litigation.

Having found a perfect way to blend her professional background, personal values, and passion for animals, Debra is unfailingly enthusiastic about her life as a mediator. "It is a phenomenally rewarding area to be involved with as a second career," she says, adding that it is a particularly strong fit for more mature adults who "know what they don't know." "As an older person, you bring a wealth of experience to the table," notes Debra. "That keeps you from being a know-it-all, because you know from your own experience that you don't know it all—and that helps you be an effective mediator."

Debra's Top Three Tips for Potential Mediators

1. **Mediation is a suitable career for people from many disciplines.** Debra was quick to point out that although it is very beneficial to be a lawyer in order to work as a mediator, you don't have to be, and she knows of therapists, psychologists, educators, and people from many different walks of life who work successfully as mediators.

2. **Find a niche.** Debra recommends that people interested in mediation find an area to specialize where they have a specific passion or expertise and then invest in quality training to enhance their skills. She chose to specialize in animal-related conflicts in part because her exposure to the professional dog show world gave her instant credibility as a mediator who understands the nature of the conflicts related to breeders and handlers.

3. **Be prepared to invest in training.** As previously noted, although a forty-hour training is the minimum requirement, you should expect to invest time and money in additional training to bring your skills up to par. Even as a trained and experienced lawyer, Debra completed two internships and multiple continuing education classes on top of the forty hours of required mediation training. In some jurisdictions, mediators may be limited with respect to the kinds of services they can provide, so it is imperative that you educate yourself about mediation regulations in the state where you plan to practice.

To learn more about mediation, consult:

- The Center for Understanding in Conflict (www.understandinginconflict.org)

- Mediate.com (www.mediate.com)

- *Success as a Mediator for Dummies* by Victoria Pynchon (Wiley, 2012)

PERFORMER

Have you been keeping your "Inner Seinfeld" hidden under your lab coat or buttoned inside your blazer? If so, now might be the perfect time to finally loosen your tie, toss off your pearls, and let the world get a taste of your more creative side!

There are dozens of ways you can profit from sharing your creative spirit on stage. Jack Turk, whom you met earlier in this chapter (page 26) does magic shows for a variety of audiences ranging from children to corporate audiences. Gilda Bonanno, whose advice was featured in the section on speakers (page 30), is part of an improvisational comedy group that performs at corporations, charity events, and comedy clubs. But of all the interesting ways that I've seen people incorporate performing into their portfolio of activities, Bob Alper just might have the most unusual story of all. He is a rabbi who traded in his pulpit for a stage, and he now claims that he is "the world's only practicing clergyman doing stand-up comedy . . . intentionally." Read on and be prepared to smile—this is a fun one.

Profile of a Stand-Up Comic—and Practicing Rabbi (Really)

"I always used a lot of humor in my rabbinate, and there is a lot of rabbi in my comedy."
—Rabbi Bob Alper

Growing up, Bob Alper found the decision to become a rabbi an easy one: the job was a good fit that allowed him to merge his desire to work with people with his strong commitment to Judaism. Bob served as a congregational rabbi for fourteen years, first in Buffalo, New York, and later in Philadelphia, Pennsylvania, while also earning a doctorate from Princeton Theological Seminary. But in 1986, after he and his wife decided that they wanted to have more time to spend at their vacation home in East Dorset, Vermont, Bob knew it was time for a change. After submitting his resignation ("I did it all properly," jokes Bob, "no scandals, same wife"), he opened an office with plans to work on a more flexible basis: officiating at lifecycle events and doing some pastoral counseling.

But less than a month after leaving his full-time position, Bob noticed an advertisement in a local paper for the Funniest Jewish Comic in Philadelphia contest. He entered the contest and came in third place behind a chiropractor and a lawyer. ("I was funnier. But who's bitter?" laughs Bob.) One of the contest judges was the host of the top-rated morning television show in Philadelphia, and she invited Bob to appear on her show. That appearance launched his career as a stand-up comedian, and within four years he was earning enough from his comedy work that he and his wife were able to move to Vermont full-time. Becoming a comic was a dream come true. "If someone had asked me what I would love to do when I was younger, I would have replied that I wanted to be a comedian," says Bob. "But the thought of making a living from doing comedy didn't seem like a possibility at the time I grew up. When the opportunity came, it was great."

Bob's training as a rabbi served him well in his development as a stand-up comic who always keeps his routines clean and appropriate. "I have this wonderful and precious title 'rabbi' that is attached to me," says Bob, "and it is always looming in the background in a very positive way. I am zealously protective of that title." His rabbinical training also comes in handy when he encounters the occasional heckler and Bob asks, "Excuse me, sir, but would you mind leading us in the silent prayer?"

Bob's brand of comedy doesn't just make his audiences laugh; it makes them think. As part of the Laugh in Peace tour, an act that has been featured on CNN and the CBS *Early Show*, he performs with a Muslim and a Baptist minister who team up in a routine that gently pokes fun at our insecurities and prejudices. When he presents his act at colleges nationwide, Bob delights in seeing Jewish and Muslim students sitting side by side, laughing and enjoying a show together. Even when he is not busy performing, Bob is able to spread his humor through his media appearances, books, tapes, and CDs—and he still works as a rabbi conducting services for the Jewish High Holy Day services in the fall.

Bob believes that making people laugh is about much more than just comedy. In his book *Life Doesn't Get Any Better than This: The Holiness of Daily Dramas* (Liguori Publications, 1996), Bob writes, "I nurture a mental treasure trove of special compliments that have followed my performances. Every entertainer does; it's a healthy way to emotionally balance the occasionally negative remarks. For example, I will never forget the woman who explained, 'Six months ago my husband died. Tonight is the first time I've laughed.' And I cherish the image passed on to me by a grateful husband about the way he and his wife smile during her chemotherapy treatments while they listen to my audio tape through headsets."

Bob is the first one to admit that his success as a comic is a bit of a rarity, especially for someone who is already well into his sixties. "Comedy is a tough business," says Bob. "A lot of really good people don't make it. Talent is not the only thing you need. I think I am a rare performer in that I like the business side of the business. I see it as a challenge."

Like every performer, Bob still has big dreams yet unfulfilled. He'd love to get on late night television. "I think I'm ready, although maybe I am too old or too Jewish," he says.

But no matter what, he just wants to do more of the same, whether it is making sad people laugh, making happy people happier, or bringing Muslim and Jewish college students together, if only for a few hours. "I'm sixty-six years old and doing well on college campuses," marvels Bob. "That's amazing, considering I am two generations older than most performers on college campuses. I mean, besides Cosby, who else is doing that? If I end up doing the same types of venues I'm currently doing for the remainder of my years, I'll be very happy."

Bob's Top Three Tips for Aspiring Comedians

1. **Find a hook.** It's helpful if you have an interesting angle to sell. Bob's dual billing as both a rabbi and a stand-up comic helps him to both attract media attention and fill his performances. "Four years in college, six years in seminary, three years in a doctoral program, and fourteen years serving a congregation—it was all because I wanted to be a comedian and I needed a hook," jokes Bob.

2. **Be persistent.** The best way to hone your craft is to just find as many audiences as you can. Offer to perform for free, and keep at it.

3. **Keep the faith.** Recognize that you will fail miserably. A lot. Everyone does.

THREE FINAL TIPS FOR CREATING INCOME FROM YOUR EXPERTISE

1. **Focus on lifestyle-friendly niches.** Think about tailoring your services to an audience whose business needs complement your lifestyle needs. For example, if you want to enjoy having your summers off, you may want to offer a service that is most in demand during the school year (for example, tutoring or piano lessons). I used this strategy early on in my coaching practice when as a young mom I wanted to be available for my children when they were home from school, and by restricting my practice to other moms, it was easier to schedule my work hours around "mommy time."

2. **Partner.** Find complementary business partners who can feed you business leads and work with you to provide services. This will reduce the amount of time you need to spend on marketing, increase your base of clients, and provide you with a network of reliable colleagues who can cover for you when you want time away from your business.

3. **Leverage your expertise with informational products.** If you are selling your expertise as a consultant, coach, or teacher, your income will be limited by your billable service hours. However, you can multiply that income by adding informational products to your line of products and services. It takes work to develop those products, but once you have created them, the opportunities for marketing them on the Internet are virtually limitless.

CHAPTER TWO

Create an Information Empire

How would you like to turn all the information you carry around inside your head into income? You can—and you don't need to be a recognized expert to do it. Thanks to an explosion in the affordability and variety of easy-to-use web-based tools and publishing platforms, there truly has never been a better time to turn your expertise into an informational product income stream. If you've ever thought about publishing a book, writing articles, making money from a blog, or selling informational products, this is the chapter for you. And even if you have never previously considered those options, this chapter will open your eyes to the growing possibilities for generating income from creating your own informational products. As you'll soon learn from the examples in this section, not everyone who produces informational products has strong writing skills. We are living at a time when people are increasingly getting their information via videos, podcasts, and webinars, and that shift has opened up opportunities for both literary types *and* nonwriters to productize their expertise into multimedia products.

I invite you to use this chapter to explore the different ways to take advantage of this monetization option, starting with the relatively new world of blogging.

BLOGGING

It wasn't all that long ago that if you wanted to create a website, you needed to pay a lot of money and hire a website designer to help do it for you. But those days are a distant memory. The new blogging platforms, such as WordPress, Blogger, and TypePad, have dramatically simplified the process of bringing a blog online; you can set up an impressive-looking and multifunctional blog in under an hour with little or no expense. That's good news, because if you plan on launching any sort of business in the near future, you will likely be building a blog as part of that venture.

Of course, launching a blog is relatively easy compared to building a blog that actually makes money. So how exactly do people make money with their blogs?

There are two ways to generate revenues from blogging: you can earn income *directly* from advertising, affiliate marketing, or sponsorships revenues, or you can create income *indirectly*, using your blog as a platform to build your brand, which in turn leads to greater interest in your products and services. Certain types of blogs tend to be better suited to the advertising model than others: sites that feature reviews of high-value products and services; sites that consistently attract repeat traffic, such as news, sports, gossip, coupon, cooking, or weather sites; and sites that cater to affluent audiences all can be good candidates for monetization.

One of the most effective ways to earn money from your blog, regardless of topic, is with affiliate advertising: a monetization model that results in referral or "thank-you" fees for recommending other people's products and services to your audience. If you've ever read a book review online, clicked on a link, and ended up purchasing the book on Amazon's sales page, there is a good possibility that the originating site earned a small affiliate fee off of your purchase. Affiliate advertising is a win-win for both you and your audience: your reader learns about valuable products and services that they might not have known about otherwise (without paying anything more in the process) and you get compensated for sharing your virtual real estate. Under the right circumstances, affiliate commissions can add up to significant income, particularly when your readers have a strong interest in the types of products you recommend. Programs that sell higher-priced digital products (webinars, training programs, and so on) can be especially attractive because many offer a 50- to 75-percent commission rate to affiliates, and those payouts can add up to hundreds or thousands of dollars in monthly commission payments for bloggers with a loyal following. Once you've built up your audience, you may be able to also secure private sponsorship deals for your blog. For example, if you write a travel blog, a cruise line or hotel may be interested in sponsoring a contest or special promotion on your site. Most experts advise that you'll need a proven track record before you can attract sizeable deals, but once you have one, those can be an attractive source of additional revenues. Of course, as with any business venture, it's not enough to just post the ads and then expect the money to roll in. It takes time to build trust with your readers. You will want to be extremely careful about who, what, and how often you choose to promote—the last thing you want to do is damage the trust of your readers by making an ill-advised recommendation.

As you can see, there are lots of different ways you might be able to create income from sponsorships and advertising on your blog. The challenge is to generate enough traffic to make that advertising worthwhile; it is a time-consuming process that takes work, dedication, and patience. It absolutely can be done, but most of you will probably find it easier to monetize your blog through these nonadvertising related methods instead:

- **Sale of informational products.** You can sell either your own products or products (webinars, e-books, and so on) from other vendors that you handpick for your audience.

- **Membership sites.** You can charge a monthly subscription fee to access a section of your site where you offer premium content to your members.

- **Speaking, consulting, coaching, and teaching offers.** Many people use their blogs as a marketing vehicle that helps to attract consulting, coaching, and teaching offers.

- **Book deals.** Did you know that the hit movie *Julie and Julia* evolved from a blog? Blogger Julie Powell's posts about her attempt to prepare all of the recipes in Julia Child's *Mastering the Art of French Cooking* caught the attention of a *New York Times* reporter, which led to a book deal that ultimately led to the movie. Although movie deals are admittedly rare, Julie Powell's book deal is not a novelty; other writers have successfully leveraged their blogs to secure book deals from major publishers. (And if you can't get a book deal, you can always compile your blog posts into a self-published book, otherwise known as a "blook.")

Whichever methods you chose for monetizing your blog, be sure to focus on a topic you really care about—and one that others care about as well. Once you've settled on your topic, you'll discover that there is no shortage of different ways you can slice and dice the type of information you share: how-to instructions, commentary, musings, links to helpful resources, product reviews, listings of events and seminars, templates, recipes, or time-sensitive offers.

THE THREE P'S OF PROFITABLE BLOG TOPICS

If you're eager to create a blog that has the potential to generate income, you'll want to give serious consideration to choosing the right focus for your site. Here are three important elements to consider:

1. **Passion.** Passion is important for two reasons. First, it is critical to pick a topic that excites you. I know that sounds painfully obvious, but you'd be amazed at the number of people who choose to write about something simply because they

{continued}

think it will make them rich. The allure of "easy income" may be sufficient fuel to get you started with a blog, but blogging is a marathon, not a sprint; successful bloggers post week after week, month after month, year after year. If you can't picture yourself writing about this same topic three years from now, find something else to blog about. Second, it is helpful to choose a topic that other people are really, really passionate about. Some of the most profitable blogs revolve around people's favorite indulgences, like cars, wine, chocolate, and designer fashion. Passion-driven blogs are relatively easy to monetize with advertising because their readers are likely to buy products, accessories, and experiences related to their passions (whether they really need them or not!).

2. **Problems.** People read blogs for information, advice, and entertainment. But they *pay* bloggers to solve their problems. Once people view you as a trusted problem solver, you'll be in a better position to monetize your site through the sale of coaching and consulting services, how-to guides, and training programs that help your readers figure out how to solve their problems more effectively.

3. **Pain.** People with problems want solutions. But people in dire pain—pending divorces, looming foreclosures, serious health issues, and the like—*need* solutions, *fast*! If you can develop products and services that provide proven and practical strategies for getting out of pain quickly, you will have a much easier time generating sales than if you focus more on preventing pain.

Remember, if you just want to blog as a means of expression, blog away. But if you eventually want to earn income from your writing, build a blog that features a mix of the three P's—passion, problems, and pain—to create a strong foundation for profitability.

Profile of a Food Blogger

"My head never stops thinking about food. I dream about food. I'll go to bed and a recipe will come to me and I'll write it down."
—Diane Eblin, health coach and blogger at www.thewholegang.org

Herndon, Virginia, resident Diane Eblin created her gluten-free food blog in 2007, shortly after her doctor informed her that she would need to switch to a gluten-free diet. She initially started the blog as a way to keep her recipes and gluten-free resources organized for her own use, but over time the blog grew into an integral component of her health coaching business. Thanks to her active online presence (her blog averages eighteen thousand views per month), Diane has been able to establish herself as an authority on gluten-free living and has enhanced her reputation as a resource for other health coaches who have clients with gluten issues. While Diane uses her blog primarily as a platform for her coaching practice, she generates some revenues from the sale of an e-cookbook and from a limited number of sponsorship arrangements with food companies. When not blogging, Diane helps her husband, Scott, run his executive coaching business, cooks, goes to yoga class, and is finishing up her studies at the Institute for Integrative Nutrition.

Diane's Eight Ingredients for Successful Blogging

1. **Learn from other bloggers.** Identify five good blogs in your niche and follow them religiously. Attract their attention by commenting on their posts. Observe the methods they use to create and maintain their audience of devoted fans.

2. **Attend blogging conferences.** Diane is a big advocate of going to blogging conferences held by organizations like BlogHer.com. She especially enjoys food blogging conferences, where she networks with other bloggers, cookbook authors, and food industry insiders. The blogging community isn't just good for business; the friends she has made at conferences have also become part of Diane's social network.

3. **Create a network of like-minded bloggers.** Diane attributes much of her success to her ever-growing network of food-related bloggers. They share information and cosponsor online blogging events that result in more traffic for all involved.

4. **Blog consistently, for search engine optimization (SEO) success.** Google rewards sites that consistently have new content; be prepared to post on a regular basis to maintain a favorable search engine ranking. Diane generally posts at least three times a week.

5. **Read for inspiration.** Coming up with new topics to blog about can get tedious, but you can gain a steady diet of inspiration from reading books, blogs, newspapers, magazines, and Twitter posts related to your field. Diane always keeps a notepad and pen by her side to capture blog inspiration when it hits.

6. **Select your blogging platform carefully.** Although it's tempting to build your blog on a free service like Blogger.com, Diane warns that you could face logistical problems if you later decide to move the blog to a platform with more robust and flexible capabilities. She is a big fan of the versatility and affordability of the WordPress publishing platform.

7. **Practice good blogging etiquette.** Bloggers share generously, but they don't take kindly to people who fail to follow good blogging etiquette (like linking back to people who link to you and giving credit where credit is due).

8. **Understand your monetization objectives.** Diane uses her blog primarily as a way to stay connected to the gluten-free community and as a means of attracting people to her coaching services. She earns some revenue from her e-cookbook and through agreements with a few select food companies. She is not a big fan of posting ads; she notes, "You need a lot of traffic to make that worthwhile."

Finally, Diane advises, "Don't be afraid to fail, and don't wait to be perfect—just start doing it!"

To learn more about blogging: There is no shortage of information about the business of blogging, but there is also no shortage of scams and unsavory operators in this space, so be careful about vetting the vendors before purchasing any of their products or advice. The more reputable vendors give away their information in abundance, so I recommend that you sign up for their free reports and teleseminars before investing in their more expensive programs. Here are three resources I have found to be especially useful:

- **Problogger.net.** Darren Rowse's book, *Problogger: Secrets for Blogging Your Way to a Six-Figure Income* (Wiley, 2010), should be required reading for anyone interested in this topic. His website is also an outstanding resource for bloggers.

- **Copyblogger.com.** This blog features useful advice about how to write clear and compelling content, along with helpful information about the business of blogs. Lots of free information on this site!

- **ThinkTraffic.net.** This site is run by Corbett Barr, who runs a number of useful sites for people who want to learn how to run a profitable blog.

DIGITAL INFORMATIONAL PRODUCTS

Constantly trading your time for money as a blogger, speaker, consultant, teacher, or coach can get tiring. And because there are only twenty-four hours in a day, there is only so much you can earn using a billable-hour model. To get yourself out of that time-for-money trap, consider turning what you know into an informational product that others can benefit from without your needing to be there. You create the product once and then continue to reap profits from the sale for as long as the market demands. That is why informational products are often referred to as passive income—although that is a bit of a misnomer, because in practice you will need to actively and consistently market the product if you want to enjoy continual sales.

There are dozens of ways to format your information into products, including audio products, mobile apps, forms and templates, bundled multiproduct programs, DVDs and videos, e-books, telecourses, workbooks, webinars, and tips booklets. Almost every day I read about another interesting informational product or package that is being sold on the Web. It never ceases to amaze me how enterprising people have become in finding novel ways to productize their expertise. Here are just three examples of ways savvy entrepreneurs are turning their knowledge into product income streams:

- The Girls' Guide to Paris (girlsguidetoparis.com) sells both mobile apps and downloadable PDFs of customized walking tours of Paris. (I couldn't resist downloading their chocolate lover's tour!) You can download one PDF for $1.98 or you can buy all ten at a significant discount. You can also sign up to be a member of their Girls' Guide to Paris Travel Club, which offers a three-tiered membership plan that ranges from a free basic service up to $575 per month for a multiservice offering.

- Nutritionist and chef Lisa Corrado (www.lisacorradonutrition .com) offers a downloadable four-week program, Ready-Set-Go! A Jump Start to Healthy Eating, for $325. The package includes four weeks of program manuals, a recipe book, daily diaries where participants can track their progress, and access to an online support community.

- Bizstarters.com, a site that provides start-up coaching, training, and resources for entrepreneurs over fifty, sells a marketing plan service ($399) that includes a downloadable marketing plan template, a one-hour telephone consultation to learn ways to improve your plan, and a final review of your revised document.

As you can see from these examples, the price point for digital products tends to be considerably higher than for paper books, especially when you start to sell bundled programs that include CDs, manuals, and audio files for several hundred dollars per package. And speaking of price points, although the prices just noted were in effect at the time this book was written, it is entirely possible that when you go to look for them the prices, or the products themselves, will have changed or even disappeared from the sites! That is one of the other benefits of creating digital products—you can alter the packaging, pricing, and product mix as often as you wish. It is a far more dynamic way to sell information than through printed products.

But as attractive as this business option appears, you can't expect to command top dollar for your products without first paying your dues; it takes time, energy, and consistent effort to build credibility with your customers. Jack Turk, the magician's marketer who you met in chapter one, says, "The dream is that you'll create a product that will sell for $200 and then you can sell a gazillion copies and the money will roll in on automatic pilot. That is not how it works. You need to create a funnel that woos the customers into buying bigger and bigger products. You want to lead the customers from a $10 report, to a $99 dollar manual, to a $500 detailed multimedia product, to a $1,000 weekend seminar, to a $5,000 ongoing coaching program. That is the real way the informational product business works."

Jack is right. And that is why most people start building their information empires in small steps. First they establish a blog, and then once they have started to build their list of interested readers, they post a simple product, like an e-book or audio file for sale. Digital downloads are the easiest informational products to create because all you need is an idea, the ability to turn a document into a PDF file, and a shopping cart service to sell the document on the web. To illustrate this point in action, let me introduce you to Pat Katepoo, a fifty-five-year-old Kaneohe, Hawaii–based woman who has been selling informational products on the Internet since the mid-1990s.

Helping People Create Flexibility, One Download at a Time

"If your informational product is born of your own experience and comes with a compelling story besides, marketing angles and media coverage will come easier."
—Pat Katepoo, founder of WorkOptions.com

Pat Katepoo runs her flexible work options advisory service, which helps professionals carve out more time for personal priorities, from her home in Hawaii. Through the widespread sales of her downloadable flexible schedule proposal packages, she has guided thousands of working mothers, boomers, and others through the successful negotiation of a flexible work arrangement. A dietitian by training, Pat never imagined that one day she would earn her living on the Internet, selling proposal packages to people around the globe. But since 1997, she has been doing just that—consistently earning a five-figure income—while selling her products to customers mainly in North America, but also in countries as far away as Australia, the United Kingdom, South Africa, and Singapore.

Of course, like most entrepreneurs, it took Pat some time to come up with her "aha!" moment. Until age thirty-one, Pat was a single working woman with a number of married friends and coworkers. When speaking with those women, Pat couldn't help but notice how hard it was on them as they tried to juggle work and family. So when Pat got married and became both a spouse and a stepparent at the same time, she was very grateful to secure a flexible professional job working just three days a week.

One day, while enjoying one of her days off, she stopped to wonder: "Why can't all my friends do this?" That question started Pat on a journey to learn everything she could about flexible work arrangements. The more she researched, the clearer it became that although there was plenty of information on the workings and value of job flexibility, there was little how-to help for people who wanted to present their case for flexibility to their employers. Interestingly, everything Pat read emphasized that the single best way to get a manager's agreement of a flexible work arrangement was to make a strong business case in a written proposal, but nobody said, "and here is *what* to say." Sensing a market need that was strongly aligned with her values, strong writing skills, and background in sales, Pat set out to create a user-friendly, flexible work proposal template. Initially she produced the template and planning tool as a small booklet that she sold locally, but as the Internet took hold in the late 1990s, she turned the booklet into a series of downloadable proposal packages and sold them on her website.

Online sales were slow at the beginning. It took a while before Pat figured out the best way to market her products, but she began to gain traction after sharing helpful articles with sites targeted to working mothers and other people interested in flexible work arrangements. Her website received favorable coverage from several media outlets including the *Wall Street Journal*, *Chicago Sun-Times*, and National Public Radio, and that media exposure, combined with the powerful testimonials from her grateful tribe of satisfied customers, has helped Pat maintain a healthy level of sales over time.

Pat's Top Three Tips for Informational Product Success

1. **Pick a nonfiction topic that solves a painful problem among a well-defined category of people.** Ideally your topic choice will reflect not only your knowledge, but also a passion. Otherwise, you'll quickly tire of both writing about it in the short term and marketing it in the long term.

2. **Be persistent.** A quality informational product takes time to write well. Expect to go through repeated cycles of rewriting and editing. Get early draft reviews from friends. Have the final draft edited by a professional copywriter or editor. Refine it yearly based on customer input. Pat's favorite guide to clearer, crisper writing is *On Writing Well* by William Zinsser (Harper Perennial, 2006).

3. **Share your positive feedback.** Ask for testimonials from early customers and get permission to post these—with their full names—on your new website. Displaying a page of success stories like these builds trust and helps promote future sales for years to come.

To learn more, look into reputable vendors of informational products like these:

- Copywriter and internet marketer Bob Bly's books, blogs, and informational products are filled with helpful information for anyone eager to learn more about blogging, info products, and effective writing (www.bly.com).

- Fred Gleek offers classes, products, and other useful information on the how-to of creating and marketing informational products (www.fredgleek.com).

- Rebecca Morgan's site, makingmoneyinjammies.com (see below), offers a good resource for learning more about creating informational products.

FIVE TIPS FROM THE MAKE MONEY IN YOUR JAMMIES EXPERT

Selling informational products can be a very lucrative endeavor. But as Rebecca Morgan, founder of the Make Money in Your Jammies e-course, says, "This is not a get-rich-quick scheme, and if anyone tells you that it is, run the other way." Morgan advises people interested in creating informational products to take these steps:

1. **Do your research before creating a product.** Consult your target market to determine whether there is a demand for your expertise before you spend a moment of time actually developing the product. Learn to use the Google AdWords tool (www.google.com/AdWords), where you can search for phrases, evaluate the market, and determine whether there is ample interest in your topic.

2. **Develop a unique spin on your topic.** Sell information that is different from all the free stuff already out there and that leverages your unique credentials and experiences.

3. **Choose a product format that is compatible with your skills.** There are lots of ways to create informational products. If you're comfortable leading a seminar, consider producing a webinar. If you're better at writing, go with e-books or print-centric products. If you hate to write, you can produce audio or video products. Don't cram yourself into a methodology that isn't a good fit with your talents and skills.

4. **Be prepared to sell.** No matter how good your product is, you need to be prepared to market it effectively.

5. **Think long term.** Although it takes a lot of up-front energy to research, write, and produce informational products, once the information is compiled, over time you'll find new ways to package and repackage it into multimedia formats.

PRINT PRODUCTS

In this chapter, I focus on downloadable products because they are relatively inexpensive and easy to produce compared to printed items. But, of course, not every informational product should be sold as a download. Lots of people prefer to read their information the "old-fashioned" way, and certain types of informational products—like posters, journals, and magnets—are, by definition, intended to be printed products. Consequently there may be times when you will need to turn to a print shop to help you bring your ideas to market.

That proved to be the case for Aileen Zsenyuk of Las Vegas, Nevada, a seventy-five-year-old great-grandmother and retired business manager for a group of physicians, who developed a product called KIT (KeepIt-Together) that helps people to organize and maintain their own set of personal medical records. Aileen came up with the idea for the KIT after she experienced a medical emergency that resulted in a sudden and unexpected hospital stay. Thanks to her experience working in a doctor's office, Aileen knew the importance of having her medical history readily available in case of an emergency, and the fact that she was able to share that information when she was hospitalized helped the doctors to quickly diagnose her condition.

After she recovered, Aileen made it her mission to share her potentially life-saving KIT with others. She spent a full year researching and designing the KIT, and along the way, consulted with her local SCORE office for advice on marketing, production, and other business-related issues. From the start, the KIT was conceived as a product intended for seniors, many of whom don't own a computer. "The seniors I know aren't really into computers that much," notes Aileen, who lives in a retirement community. The KIT comes packaged in a compartmentalized portfolio and includes a wallet-sized medical ID card, an in-case-of-emergency medical record form designed to be posted on the refrigerator, and a fill-in-the-blank booklet where people can record their personal and family medical histories. (The KIT is sold online at www.medicalrecordorganizer.com.)

Aileen used a local printer to produce the kits. "They were so helpful all along the way," said Aileen, clearly grateful to have worked with a local vendor who took a personal interest in her product. Aileen recommends that if you want to sell your product in a printed format, it pays to get price quotes from several sources. Although online print vendors might be less expensive, price is only one factor to consider. An experienced local printer, particularly one with significant design experience, can be a critical ally in helping you develop a winning product. They may be able to both suggest ways to cut costs and help you improve the product design, and they also may work with you to market the product locally.

BOOK PUBLISHING

Even as recently as five years ago, I might not have chosen to include book publishing as a realistic income option for semi-retirement; landing a publisher was simply too tough a hurdle for most people to clear. But times have changed, and now—as a result of the proliferation of self-publishing tools, print-on-demand technologies, and inexpensive author support services—the playing field is open for anyone willing to put in the time and effort to produce a book for sale. Given all the publishing options, selecting the best method for publishing your book—traditional publisher, e-publisher, or printing services—can be a project in and of itself. Each of the publishing models offers advantages and drawbacks, and what appears to be the best option today may be different by next year. Here is a brief comparison of the relative merits of traditional publishing versus self-publishing:

Traditional Publishing

Benefits:

- The publisher oversees the book from concept to market (editing, design, distribution, marketing, and so on).

- The publisher absorbs all costs of publication and arranges to get the book into all the appropriate distribution channels and retail outlets. The author is paid an advance against royalties prior to the book's publication (the author keeps the advance regardless of sales).

- The author enjoys the prestige and credibility associated with being an author "accepted" by a traditional publisher—a stamp of approval that can be used to attract more lucrative business opportunities.

- Publishing companies, particularly the larger ones, have greater clout when it comes to the distribution and marketing of the book.

Challenges:

- The author needs to secure a book agent and write a book proposal in order to even be considered by most traditional publishers. (Some smaller publishers will accept proposals submitted directly by an author, though.)

- Publishers want to work with authors who already have an established platform and media presence; simply having a great idea is not enough to secure a contract.

- The time lapse between submitting a manuscript and actual publication can be significantly longer than with digital publishing, which can be a liability for authors writing about time-sensitive topics.

- The publishing company retains the majority of the revenues associated with the sale of your book.

Self-Publishing

Benefits:

- The author maintains complete editorial control over the finished product (and there is no need to prepare a proposal or secure a book agent).

- The time it takes to bring a book from manuscript to market is much shorter than traditional publishing; print-on-demand technology allows authors to literally publish overnight.

- There are a growing number of "one-stop-shop" services available to help authors with every aspect of the book publishing process: from editing to layout to cover design to proofreading.

- The author retains all profits from the book (after absorbing the costs of editing, design, production, printing, fulfillment, and marketing).

Challenges:

- Because the author is responsible for every aspect of the book— from writing to marketing—this can be an overwhelming do-it-yourself project, particularly for first-time authors.

- This project could result in a negative cash flow (and a garage full of unsold books).

- Self-publishing still lacks some of the cachet and credibility associated with books published by a major publisher. This can be an issue if you want to use the book to attract attention in academia and/or corporate markets, although this tends to be less of a problem in other markets.

Whichever method of publishing you choose, be aware that publishing is not a get-rich-quick scheme. As much as I'd love to say otherwise, very few authors make serious money directly from the sale of their books. Although it is difficult to find firm statistics, it appears that most earn less than $5,000 per book *before* expenses. Sadly, many great writers are not great marketers, and successful publishing often comes down to effective marketing. Of course, there are authors who make a solid living pumping out one or two books a year, or by selling in bulk to companies and associations, but for most people, especially nonfiction authors, the financial benefits of publishing come primarily from lucrative speaking engagements, consulting assignments, and higher coaching fees that the author commands as a result of the book.

In spite of the challenges, there are still many compelling reasons to publish a book. Even with all the other media out there, or perhaps because of it, the prestige associated with "being the author of" is hard to replicate with other informational product formats. Publishing a book, especially in business circles, can open doors to opportunities that might have previously been out of reach. The process of researching and writing the book can increase your knowledge base and make you an expert in your field. And on a personal level, most authors find tremendous satisfaction in publishing a book: it can be a meaningful way to leave a legacy, share new ideas, or contribute to the greater good.

To learn more: Not surprisingly, there are numerous books, websites, and informational products available to help people learn about all aspects of the publishing world. Here are some of the resources I have found helpful in my own publishing endeavors:

- **Websites for writers.** There are lots of websites for people interested in writing books, but I think the best place to start is with a visit to WritersDigest.com. *Writers Digest* has been around for over ninety years (originally in print format), and they are considered the destination site for writers who want to hone their craft and learn the business. Here are a few more helpful sites:

    Gotham Writers Workshops (www.writingclasses.com) and Media Bistro (www.mediabistro.com) both host reputable training programs for writers.

    Self-Publishing Resources (www.selfpublishingresources.com) was created by Marilyn and Tom Ross, whose books about self-publishing are industry classics.

- **Print-on-demand services.** It's amazing what you can learn about print-on-demand simply by visiting the websites of the major print-on-demand services, including Amazon's CreateSpace (www.createspace.com), Lulu (www.lulu.com), and Lightning Source (www1.lightningsource.com). They are great resources for educating yourself about the features, benefits, and costs associated with this publishing platform.

- **Local resources.** Your local library or community college may offer introductory classes about book publishing and book marketing. Explore the possibility of joining a writers' group to hone your writing skills.

FREELANCE WRITING

Finally, if you love to write but don't want to get involved with publishing products, then you might want to explore freelance writing. Possibilities for freelance writing include the following:

- **Writing "ghost" blog posts.** Many business owners want to have a blog, but they have neither the time nor the inclination to write their own blog posts. As a result, there is a market for freelance blog writers. Newbie bloggers typically start at the low end of the pay scale (under $50 per post), but seasoned bloggers and people with a strong technical or industry expertise can command several hundred dollars per post. Sites that post blogging jobs include ProBlogger (jobs.problogger.net), BloggingPro (bloggingpro.com/jobs), and Blogger Jobs (www.bloggerjobs.biz). In addition, you can find such positions listed on major job boards like Indeed (www.indeed.com) and Career Builder (www.careerbuilder.com).

- **Business writing.** Companies, associations, and nonprofits utilize freelance writers to produce content for their newsletters, websites, and other publications. They also hire writers to craft speeches, write position papers, issue press releases, and develop marketing collateral. These jobs are especially well suited for people who have a combination of strong industry expertise and good writing skills.

- **Technical writing.** Whenever any new product involving technology is released to the market, there is a need for some type of brochure or material to explain it. Technical writers who possess the combination of strong writing skills and the ability to explain complicated concepts in easy-to-understand language—along with strong technical, scientific, or financial expertise—can command a high rate for their in-demand talents.

- **Magazines and newspapers.** Freelance writers get paid to write articles for popular magazines, trade journals, and newspapers. Newspapers and websites hire subject matter experts to write columns, provide commentary, and respond to readers' questions.

As you review this list, think about ways you might be able to use your unique industry expertise and insider knowledge to your competitive advantage. Then spend some time exploring the many resources and courses available to help you learn about the world of freelance writing.

To learn more, in addition to the resources already mentioned in this section, here are some of my favorites:

- The Well-Fed Writer (www.wellfedwriter.com) is a site targeted for business writers.

- The American Medical Writers Association (www.amwa.org) and the Society for Technical Communication (www.stc.org) are appropriate for technical writers.

- Freelance Writing Jobs (www.freelancewritinggigs.com) is a useful site for finding freelance job leads, writing tips, and business advice.

THREE FINAL TIPS ON CREATING AN INFORMATION EMPIRE

1. **Focus on producing "how-to" information.** There is an almost limitless appetite for "how-to" information, and as long as you can explain things in a clear, organized, and practical style, you don't need to be an exceptionally great writer to make money from your informational products. Your buyers will be more interested in your expertise than in your literary talents.

2. **Try things out with a blog first.** Writing a blog is an easy way to test out your writing chops; you can blog in small increments, change things up depending on your mood, and use the blog as a way to gauge reader's interest in your expertise.

3. **Take advantage of free teleclasses, downloadable reports, and seminars.** I have been amazed by the high quality of the free introductory teleclasses, downloads, and seminars presented online by the different sites that are selling services in the informational product and blogging space. Granted, there are some that are little more than thinly-veiled sales pitches, but in general, you can learn a surprising amount about a number of business-related topics without ever paying a dime. These classes are filled with useful information and provide a helpful way to vet vendors before you invest in their more expensive educational products or services.

CHAPTER THREE

Start a Small Service Business

This next chapter is for all of you who would prefer to find a way to make money that doesn't require you to make speeches, write books, or teach. Clearly not everyone is cut out for life as an "expert," and fortunately there is plenty of demand for people who want to run other types of businesses. One of the easiest ways to do this is with a service-based business that helps companies and people with the day-to-day demands of their lives. For lack of a more technical term, I refer to these as the let-me-help-make-your-life-easier category of businesses: a variety of services that alleviate the pain, drudgery, and worry associated with the endless chores we all juggle on a daily basis.

Here are five reasons why service businesses are a particularly good fit for people looking for a lifestyle-friendly career during semi-retirement:

1. **Low start-up expenses.** Small service businesses require little start-up capital compared to brick-and-mortar businesses; you probably already own the basic equipment and tools you'll need, your marketing expenses should be minimal, and in most cases you won't require much additional training to do your job well.

2. **Built-in repeat business.** There will likely be an ongoing demand for your services—dogs must be walked every day, the elderly need rides to appointments several times a week, and self-employment taxes need to be filed on a quarterly basis. As a result, after you have secured a steady stream of customers, you can reduce the time you spend on marketing efforts and increase your billable working hours. Spreading the word about your services will happen organically. Once people find a reliable provider, they are more than happy to share your name with friends—Glen tells Lindsey, who tells Bruce, who tells Grace—and before you know it, you've got a full roster of satisfied clients.

3. **Life experience—a valued asset.** Local services businesses are a natural fit for "older" people who bring a lifetime of experiences—raising children, caring for pets, running homes, and dealing with aging parents—to their work. Personal qualities that tend to come easily to people over fifty, like maturity, a strong work ethic, and empathy are also highly valued and appreciated.

4. **A lifestyle-friendly pursuit.** Although not all service businesses can be run on a flexible basis, the ones highlighted in this chapter can largely be operated on a more part-time schedule.

5. **A scalable business.** Service businesses are relatively easy to scale up or down; you can start your business with a handful of customers and then choose to grow the business as time and resources allow.

All of these features combine to make service businesses an appealing, albeit not always terribly glamorous, income option. Please be aware that many of these opportunities are subject to zoning, licensing, and insurance restrictions, so always do your homework and file the needed paperwork before opening for business.

HANDYMAN OR HANDYWOMAN SERVICES

If you have a knack for fixing, repairing, or sprucing things up around the house, you can build a business around your fix-it talents. In most communities, there is an inexhaustible demand for people to complete basic repair jobs, small painting projects, and other tasks on the "Honey-do!" list. Although it might seem like people should be able to do these jobs themselves, the reality is that lots of people—the elderly, two-career couples, and people with two left thumbs—simply lack the time, tools, and desire to take care of these tasks on their own. You can offer your services on an as-needed basis, or you can sell packaged services to maximize your profits. For instance, if you live in an area where winters are harsh, you could offer snowbird services for absentee homeowners; if you live near a retirement community, you could market a "move-in" service helping people to install computers, hang pictures, and assemble furniture; and during December you could sell a holiday package that includes the delivery and disposal of Christmas trees, hanging of holiday lights, and display of holiday decorations.

In general, marketing this line of work tends to be a low-budget affair; you don't need to invest in a fancy website or a big advertising campaign to attract clients. This is a business that depends heavily on word of mouth and personal referrals, so the best marketing technique of all is to consistently deliver a quality service at a fair price. It also helps to spend time at networking events where people can meet you and see that you are the type of person they would be comfortable inviting into their homes.

PERSONAL SUPPORT SERVICES

Life is hectic, especially for time-starved working parents and busy executives, and there never seem to be enough hours in the day to handle all the chores that need attention. As a result, there is a need for outside vendors to do the many things people don't have time to do themselves: tasks like grocery shopping, paying bills, waiting for delivery people, and picking up prescriptions. If you are the type of person who loves to run errands, organize clutter, or assist people in need, here are some variations of personal support services you could offer:

- **Concierge services.** Hotels have long provided concierge services to their guests, but in recent years this service has expanded to hospitals, office complexes, and residential living communities. Concierge literally means "keeper of the keys," and as a concierge you'll help your clients locate tickets to sold-out shows, arrange for limousines, make last-minute dinner reservations, and otherwise make the impossible, possible. People who work as concierges for companies or residence centers may also plan day trips, golf outings, and holiday events. Although many concierges do work on a full-time basis, people who run their own concierge services tend to work on a more flexible schedule. To learn more about this career, consult the National Concierge Association at www.ncakey.com or *Entrepreneur* magazine's start-up business guide for people interested in creating their own concierge service, www.entrepreneur.com.

- **Postpartum doula.** The first few weeks following childbirth can be a stressful time for new parents. For past generations, family was almost always on hand to help out, but in today's world, many new parents don't have family living nearby. This has created the need for postpartum doulas—trained helpers who provide assistance with breastfeeding support, cooking, light housekeeping, and other household-related chores. Doulas may work independently or through an agency, and assignments last anywhere from a few days to a few weeks. To learn more about this profession and options for certification, consult DONA International, the world's oldest and largest doula association at www.dona.org.

- **Personal chef.** Busy people don't have the energy or time to cook dinner every night, but they still want to enjoy nutritious and tasty home-cooked meals. If you love to cook, consider investing in a career as a personal chef who plans menus, shops, and prepares customized meals for one or more client households. In addition to providing in-home personal chef services, you could also cater small dinner parties, office luncheons, or small charity events. Keep in mind that because you will be working with food, it is imperative that you check out licensing and zoning requirements before you hang out your shingle for business. To learn more, consult the United States Personal Chef Association at www.uspca.com.

- **Personal shopper.** Shopping is a favorite leisure activity for many of us. But did you know that some people actually get paid to shop for busy families, wealthy people, and companies? Personal shoppers help people who either don't have time to shop or lack confidence in their ability to select the "perfect" gift or outfit. If you love to shop and have impeccable taste, this could be a really fun way to profit from your passion. To learn more, look into the Association of Image Consultants International at www.aici.org or take a look at the *How to Become a Personal Shopper* guides sold at Fabjob.com or Entrepreneur.com.

- **Driving services.** People hire drivers for all different reasons: executives need transportation to the airport, parents need children shuttled to after-school activities, and seniors need help getting to and from doctor's appointments. If you have a comfortable car, a friendly disposition, appropriate insurance coverage, and a clean driving record, you could offer your driving services as a budget-friendly alternative to the pricier commercial limousine and town car companies. Or if you own a truck, you could do dump runs or assist with small local moving jobs. Most people advertise this type of business using inexpensive marketing strategies like posting flyers on local bulletin boards and word-of-mouth referrals.

- **Professional organizer.** If you have a flair for organizing data, cleaning clutter, or making order out of chaos, a career as a professional organizer might be a smart match for you. Organizers help people clean out cluttered garages, organize files, and set up more efficient billing systems. Many professional organizers have a recurring schedule of services that they bill their clients for on a monthly basis. To learn more, consult the National Association of Professional Organizers at www.napo.net; they offer a number of helpful training programs and resources.

SENIOR CARE SERVICES

More people are living longer than ever before, and with over seventy-six million baby boomers approaching retirement, the demand for eldercare services is certain to explode. Many seniors need help with both the basic tasks of daily living and the administrative needs connected to estate planning, medical claims filing, and bill paying. If you enjoy working with people in the same age group as yourself (give or take a few years), here are three ways you can turn that interest into a business:

- **Senior move managers.** Senior move managers help people juggle all the issues involved with cleaning out their homes and relocating to a new residence. Additionally, they work with individuals who choose to stay in their own homes but need help streamlining their possessions and organizing their space. This is a business where your older age will work in your favor; according to a survey conducted by the National Association of Senior Move Managers (NASMM) in 2010, 75 percent of their members are age fifty or older. To learn more, visit www.nasmm.org.

- **Medical claims assistance professional.** As most of us know from personal experience, dealing with medical insurance claims can be a massive headache, and if handled incorrectly, you can lose a lot of money needlessly. Medical claims assistance professionals help people negotiate through the medical insurance system: they file and track claims, check the accuracy of bills, and advocate on their clients' behalf when negotiating claims with insurance companies. Although there is currently no certification needed in this field, most claims assistance professionals have previously worked for insurance providers or in a doctor's office and/or have extensive personal experience in this arena. To learn more, consult the Alliance of Claims Assistance Professionals at www.claims.org.

- **Geriatric care managers.** If you have a background as a nurse, social worker, gerontologist, or other professional involved with eldercare, you might want to explore options to become a geriatric care manager who assists seniors (or their family members) with making decisions regarding long-term healthcare and living arrangements. Care managers visit their clients in their homes, assess their needs, arrange for care services, and monitor ongoing care. In addition, they can be a resource for families of older adults and others with chronic needs, including those suffering from Alzheimer's and other dementia conditions or Parkinson's disease. Care managers can work independently, freelance through an agency, or be employed by a larger senior care or residential institution. For more information about this career, including certification options, consult the National Association of Professional Geriatric Care Managers at www.caremanager.org.

Turning Clutter Into Cash: Profile of a Senior Move Manager

"At age sixty-eight, I am a comfort to other people precisely because I am not a kid."
—Beth Chapman, senior move manager

For nearly twenty years, Beth Chapman worked as a public relations consultant to the financial services industry, helping to develop public relations and marketing programs. But when the 2008 financial crisis took a heavy toll on her clients, she began to look for other opportunities outside of the financial services world. A friend who knew Beth was exploring new careers sent her a newspaper article about senior move managers who help people manage the daunting process of downsizing and moving to a new residence.

Beth was intrigued by the idea for several reasons. She had been wanting to start a business that would serve the large population of retirees where she lived in Cape Cod, Massachusetts; she liked the fact that it wouldn't take much capital to get a business like this started; and because she had personally moved homes eighteen times, settled five estates, and served as the chairperson of her church's white elephant sale, she knew she had the experience needed to succeed as a move manager. After going online and reading about the annual conference of the National Association of Senior Move Managers (NASMM), Beth was sold on the concept. "I wanted to attend every seminar they were offering," recalls Beth. "That for me was the key deciding factor."

She flew out to the conference and, as anticipated, had a wonderful time meeting people and learning about the industry. The people she met came from a wide variety of backgrounds as social workers, home stagers, and movers. They had more years than Beth in the moving industry, but few of them had much experience with public relations. The more she networked, the more Beth began to realize that there could be an opportunity to both start her own senior move manager business *and* help other senior move managers publicize their businesses too.

While mulling over the possibilities for teaching PR to her peers, Beth set about building her own senior move business, Extra Daughters (www.extradaughters.com), a service to help people in her community declutter, organize, and relocate. As part of her offerings, she developed a Life Legacy Party, a system that helps clients to inventory their "treasures" and then distribute them in an orderly, fair, and meaningful way to family and friends. As she built her business, Beth tried out different types of marketing and advertising strategies and kept notes on which strategies worked best. She discovered that some of her most effective advertising tools were decidedly low-tech techniques, such as posting flyers on bulletin boards. The homespun feel of her local community outreach seems to resonate with this demographic more effectively than a glitzier marketing campaign. "Bulletin boards are big," says Beth, noting that more than three-quarters of her inquiries come from bulletin boards. She also bought vinyl letters for her car, registered it as a commercial vehicle, and turned it into a moving billboard. "I get comments all the time," laughs Beth. "It is a low-budget way to market."

Beth is already looking forward to attending her next NASMM conference, but at that event she will do double-duty as both an attendee and a presenter speaking about public relations strategies. By that time, she will have tested out many of her suggestions in her own business, and she thinks that real-world experience will boost her credibility with her audience. Beth hopes that the conference will serve as a launch pad for what she terms a "new branch" of her public relations services. "I am focusing on the Big M's: money and moving," says Beth, who plans to continue to work with her financial service clients along with her new senior move manager clients.

Assuming that this new branch of her business takes off, Beth plans to hire people to assist with the hands-on tasks of Extra Daughters—a task she anticipates should prove easy, given all the retirees in her town. She readily admits that she has a lot on her plate, but she insists she would not do it any other way. "My bottom line is that if you've got the energy and you're not done yet, then do something you'll really enjoy. You probably have already paid your dues doing jobs you don't really like much," says Beth. "At this stage in your life, you don't have time to do that again."

Beth's Top Three Tips for Potential Senior Move Managers

1. **Attend the NASMM national conference.** The conference is a wonderful way to learn and meet your industry peers.

2. **Partner with complementary service providers.** Go to the local senior living facilities in your area and speak with them to see if you can help their residents with their relocations. (Some facilities offer this service as a "gift" to entice prospects to become new residents.)

3. **Use your age to your advantage.** "I had no qualms age-wise about doing this; I relate well to this population," says Beth.

PERSONAL/HOME IMPROVEMENT SERVICES

For better or worse, we live in a world where appearances matter. It can make the difference between success and failure in many different situations, whether it is a job interview, a first date, or an important business meeting. And because image is so important, people are willing to pay good money for assistance in this area. If you are someone with impeccable taste, savvy style, flawless manners, or a great eye for design, here are some ways you could turn your personal panache into profits:

- **Image consultant.** Image consultants teach people how to present themselves in the best light possible. They help people choose the most flattering clothing, show them how to apply make-up, and advise them on selecting attractive accessories. Many image consultants also offer personal shopping and wardrobe consultation services. Some image consultants specialize in meeting the needs of specific niche populations such as business executives, celebrities, or politicians—or people who have special wardrobe challenges because they are full-figured, petite, or tall. Image consultants are hired by both individuals and organizations to provide seminars and coaching services. To learn more about how to train as an image consultant, consult the Association of Image Consultants International at www.aici.org.

- **Etiquette or protocol consultant.** Are you a fan of Emily Post? If so, you may be able to turn your passion for etiquette into profits. Companies hire protocol consultants to teach their executives about the norms and customs of other cultures; parents pay to have their children schooled in the social graces of everyday table manners, proper telephone etiquette, and other social niceties; and universities hire consultants to teach business etiquette to their graduating students. To learn more, consult the International Association of Protocol Consultants and Officers at www.protocolconsultants.org, or explore the different etiquette classes offered by the Emily Post Institute at www.emilypost.com.

- **Home staging services.** Home stylists and staging professionals help people beautify their homes by rearranging furniture, adding accessories, and making other small changes that enhance the visual appeal of the house in a budget-friendly way. This is an especially useful service for people who are trying to sell their homes since stagers know how to "neutralize" a home's appearance in order to improve the likelihood of a sale. No advanced degree is necessary for this occupation; people with a flair for design can become stylists without any training or certifications. If you want to get training, there are a number of workshops and products to help you learn about this business. For more information, consult www.redecorate.com or www.stagedhomes.com.

BUSINESS SUPPORT SERVICES

Most small companies these days run "lean and mean"; consequently they tend to outsource their administrative, technical, and bookkeeping tasks to freelance service providers. If you have strong business, financial, or technical support skills, this can be a good way to use your skills without having to drag yourself into an office every day. Here are several ways to potentially earn a living in the business services field:

- **Virtual assistant (VA).** Virtual assistants support business people with their administrative, creative, and technical needs. They provide a convenient solution for the growing population of home-based entrepreneurs who have periodic needs for assistance, but can't justify the cost of hiring a full-time support person. If you have a background as an administrative assistant or strong office skills, life as a VA is an attractive option to consider. Unlike traditional administrative workers who must commute to an office, most VAs work remotely from their own home office locations, handling tasks including correspondence, data entry, billing, and making travel arrangements. For more information, consult the International Virtual Assistants Association at www.ivaa.org.

- **Bookkeeper.** Many entrepreneurs lack the inclination and time to keep their own financial records. But like it or not, bookkeeping is one of those tasks that has to be done, and that drives a strong demand for freelance bookkeepers. Bookkeepers' duties can range from minimal record-keeping responsibilities to handling all tasks leading up to the preparation of financial statements and tax forms. Even if you have no prior experience as a bookkeeper, you can learn these skills fairly quickly; many community colleges and distance learning programs offer basic bookkeeping classes that prepare you to take the National Certified Bookkeeping Exam. Although certification is not required, this credential is very helpful to distinguish you from the competition. To learn more, consult the American Institute of Professional Bookkeepers at www.aipb.org or the National Association of Certified Professional Bookkeepers at www.nacpb.org.

- **Editor or Proofreader.** As more of our communication takes place via e-mail and the Internet, there will be a continuing need for people with strong editing and proofreading skills. Anyone who publishes content, maintains a web presence, or sends correspondence is a potential client, but the demand is especially strong among professionals who routinely produce a large volume of content, such as bloggers, lawyers, and publishers. To learn more about this career, consult the Editorial Freelancers Association at www.the-efa.org and the National Association of Independent Writers and Editors at naiwe.com.

- **Translator.** As the United States becomes an increasingly multilingual nation, the need for qualified translators will continue to grow. Doctors, lawyers, insurance agents, and other professionals who routinely deal with the public need help translating correspondence and documents for their multicultural customer base. Although the market is currently strongest for Spanish-speaking translators, there is also a demand for people who can translate other languages including Chinese and Arabic. You can learn more at the American Translators Association website, www.atanet.org, and you'll also find translation opportunities posted on many of the major job boards.

PET CARE SERVICES

People love their pets, sometimes as much as or more than they love their own children! According to the National Pet Owners Survey sponsored by the American Pet Products Association, Americans spent over $50 *billion* on their beloved pets in 2011. Although much of that money was spent on food and healthcare, there is still plenty being spent on pet pampering and pet care services. If you're a die-hard pet lover, here are some lifestyle-friendly career choices to explore:

- **Doggie daycare.** At a time when so many people are working long hours, the demand for doggie daycare services is on the rise. As a daycare provider, you will be responsible for feeding, walking, and playing with the dogs while their owners are busy at work. Whether you choose to run a daycare service out of your home, through a franchise, or at a leased business location, you'll likely find plenty of customers eager to use your services, although you should be aware that the demand for your services is likely to be greatest during the summer months and peak vacation times, so this could put a crimp in your personal travel plans. For more information about careers in doggie daycare, consult Pet Sitters International at www.petsit.com.

- **Dog walking.** Dog walking is an easy business to start, a great excuse to get exercise, and a surprisingly lucrative enterprise for people who work in major cities (some New York City–based dog walkers earn in excess of six figures annually, although they are admittedly a rarity). Start-up costs are minimal, and it can be relatively easy to build up a steady stream of clients after you establish yourself as a caring, trustworthy, and reliable provider. Believe it or not, you can even get certified in this line of work by attending the Dog Walking Academy, a four-day intensive training workshop designed to equip you to start your own dog walking business. You can learn more about the Academy and other dog-related business opportunities at www.dogtec.org.

- **Pet photography.** Pets are an integral part of the family, so it's no surprise that an increasing number of people are willing to pay for professional portraits of their four-legged friends. And it's not just dogs and cats who are posing for portraits. Equine photography is a growing subset of the pet photography business, with opportunities to find business at horse shows, race tracks, and equestrian centers. To learn more about business opportunities as a photographer, check out Virtual Photography Studio at virtualphotographystudio.com.

- **Pet paraphernalia.** From Halloween outfits to gourmet biscuits to eco-friendly bath products, pet owners are eager to indulge their furry friends with special toys and treats. You can sell your goodies at craft shows and local pet stores or on the Internet. If you don't want to create your own products, consider becoming an independent sales rep for one of the direct sales/home party companies that specialize in pet-related products (check the Direct Selling Association at www.dsa.org for listings).

- **Grooming services.** Nothing spruces up a pet's appearance quite like a good shower and shave—so to speak. Pet grooming services can be operated in stores, private homes, salons, and in mobile pet grooming vans. If you are leery about creating a pet grooming business of your own, investigate the options for buying into a pet grooming franchise (for listings, check www.entrepreneur.com).

To learn more about careers and business opportunities in the pet arena, consult these websites:

- The American Society for the Prevention of Cruelty to Animals offers a wealth of information at www.aspca.org/about-us/faq/animal-careers.aspx.

- DogTec.org: This site has a number of excellent articles and training resources for people interested in starting a pet business.

As you can see, the options for turning your passion for animals into profits are many and varied. And if this niche intrigues you, I can think of no better way to demonstrate how you can turn your love of pets into a full-fledged business than to introduce you to Sharon Sakson. I spoke with Sharon right before Thanksgiving 2011 and was delighted to discover that among her many different income streams, she helps coproduce the televised broadcast of the Kennel Club of Philadelphia dog show on Thanksgiving Day, the most viewed dog show of the year. As you'll soon learn, Sharon has turned her lifelong passion for dogs into a robust and multifaceted income portfolio.

Portrait of a Dog Lover Extraordinaire

"I absolutely love my work. It is the most wonderful thing in the world."
—Sharon Sakson

Many of us love our dogs. But Sharon Sakson doesn't just love dogs; she has built an impressive career around that passion. As was the case for many of the second-act stories featured in this book, it took a while before Sharon was able to craft a career around her passion. After graduating from college, she settled into the broadcast news world with jobs that included a field production assignment with *ABC Nightly News* anchor Peter Jennings. Life in the news world was hectic, but even with her packed schedule, Sharon always found a way to spend time with her dogs. In addition to keeping dogs as pets, she worked as a breeder, participated in dog shows, and studied to become an accredited American Kennel Club (AKC) dog show judge.

All went well until the economic downturn of 2008 when Sharon lost her job. At the time, she was just fifty-six years old, and at a point when she was neither financially nor emotionally ready to retire. Fortunately it didn't take Sharon long to reconfigure her dog-related hobbies into work that generated a full-time income—a multipronged career that takes advantage of her passion in a variety of interesting ways. Although the transition was a difficult one, Sharon says she now finds herself busier and happier then ever.

Today she travels the world as an AKC international dog show judge and has visited numerous countries including Canada, England, France, Italy, Switzerland, Germany, Russia, Finland, and Taiwan. She also works as a breeder of champion whippets and Brussels griffons, and although the income she earns as a breeder is relatively low, it helps to offset the considerable costs of caring for and showing her dogs in competitions. While at those competitions, she is able to network with other judges and handlers, and just as with any other profession, the more people she meets, the more opportunities for judging come her way.

In addition to her breeding and judging activities, Sharon writes about dogs. She is a contributing columnist to *Dog News* magazine and the author of several books about dogs, including: *Paws & Effect: The Healing Power of Dogs* (Spiegel & Grau, 2009), *Paws to Protect: Dogs Saving Lives and Restoring Hope* (Alyson Publications, 2008) and *Paws & Reflect: The Special Bond Between Man and Dog* (Alyson Publications, 2008). Her books feature heartwarming stories about dogs as healers, rescuers, and faithful companions. But unlike so many other books in this genre, hers are more than just feel-good stories; Sharon includes scientific studies and research to substantiate her claims about the human-like qualities of the featured dogs. Sharon also earns income from speaking engagements and offering private consulting services to help dog owners with their dog-related behavioral issues and questions.

In between juggling her many income-generating activities, Sharon always makes time to relax and enjoy her household full of dogs. At the time we spoke, she was caring for eight dogs and a litter of six puppies, a task that some would consider a full-time job all its own. (Not surprisingly, our interview was interrupted several times by the sound of dogs barking in the background!) She is also involved with Xolos for Chronic Pain Relief, a nonprofit organization that matches Xolo puppies, a unique therapeutic dog breed, with patients suffering from chronic pain conditions. And finally, as if that was not enough to keep her busy, Sharon continues to do television production work on a freelance basis whenever time allows.

Sharon's Top Three Tips to Profit from Your Pet Passions

1. **Familiarize yourself with the American Kennel Club's offerings.**
   The AKC website www.akc.org, is an outstanding resource for breeders and dog lovers.

2. **Be prepared to work hard (and long) to train as an AKC judge.**
   Although dog judging may seem simple to the untrained eye, judges have to meet the exceedingly rigorous standards set by the American Kennel Club. These include a minimum of twelve years' involvement in the diverse field of dog competitions, breeding of at least five litters of champion dogs, and successful completion of a series of examinations. To learn more, consult www.akc.org.

3. **Network.** Networking is as important in the dog world as it is in the business world. Sharon's diverse income streams provide her with opportunities to attend different events where she can continually make new acquaintances, and that, in turn, has helped expand her income potential.

THREE FINAL TIPS FOR PEOPLE INTERESTED IN PURSUING A SERVICE BUSINESS

1. **Don't underestimate the value of your talents.** Most of us have a tendency to underestimate the true worth of our skills and experiences. But keep in mind that what may come naturally to you may not come so naturally to others. You might think nothing of your ability to easily cook nutritious and tasty meals, but to the person who eats on the run and is craving a healthy alternative, that skill can be invaluable.

2. **Be honest about your lifestyle objectives.** Define what a good work-life balance means to you before investing money in a business. If you really want to work only ten

{continued}

hours a week, you don't want to work weekends, and you have no interest in doing much marketing, you need to focus on service businesses where those time constraints won't be a major problem. This doesn't mean you lack ambition; it simply means you're being honest about how much work you can comfortably handle. Some of these businesses require you to be on call and respond to emergencies, whereas others can be done on a by-appointment-only basis. Pick and choose accordingly.

3. **Write a basic business plan.** No matter how big or small your potential business, it's a good idea to write a basic business plan. It doesn't have to be anything lengthy or fancy; think of a business plan as a roadmap that outlines what your business is, where you plan to go with it, and how you plan to get there. It is a fluid document that can (and should) be amended as time goes on. For help with the basics of writing a business plan, consult your local SBA or SCORE office.

CHAPTER FOUR

Pursue a Business-in-a-Box Opportunity

If the thought of creating your own business from scratch makes you uncomfortable, you may instead want to consider a business-in-a-box opportunity, such as a franchise, direct sales, or licensing arrangement. When you invest in a business-in-a-box, you eliminate many of the headaches associated with starting your own company. Instead of having to create your business from the ground up, you get to take advantage of a proven and successful business model; they've already worked out the kinks, developed best practices, and built the infrastructure for you. Of course, there is a price tag associated with this level of convenience. The cost of buying into a business-in-a-box model ranges from a few hundred dollars for a simple starter kit to hundreds of thousands of dollars for a more elaborate franchise.

In this chapter, you'll learn about four different types of business-in-a-box opportunities: direct sales, franchises, licensing agreements, and business start-up kits. I've also included a fifth option—selling through online marketplaces such as eBay—because, although technically not a business-in-a-box model, it offers you much of the same support, community, and infrastructure as a business-in-a-box system.

You'll be pleasantly surprised by the range of possibilities in our global economy—the options available today are far greater than just McDonald's or Amway.

DIRECT SALES COMPANIES

I suspect more than one of you will read this title, roll your eyes, and think, "Really, Nancy? You are going to try to convince me to become an Avon salesperson? C'mon now!" I hear you. Like many people, I used to think direct sales was a career best suited for stay-at-home moms or for people who couldn't find a "real" job. I equated direct sales with one of two things: unscrupulous pyramid schemes and unwanted invitations to home parties where I'd be pressured to buy products I didn't want, like, or need. Even worse, once I was at the party, I would be asked to sit through a sales pitch to learn about "an opportunity of a lifetime" guaranteed to make me millions. Ugh!

But over time I've met too many impressive people who are successfully working in direct sales to continue to dismiss this business model as a second-rate alternative. Most direct sales people aren't misinformed zealots; they are professionals who are genuinely enthused about their careers and earning potential (much more so than many of my corporate clients). A career in direct sales is not for everyone. But for the right person, with the right set of skills, working for the right company, this can be a good flexible work solution. Here are some of the reasons why:

- **Low barriers to entry.** Direct sales companies provide you with the inventory, marketing materials, and forms you need to begin selling from the day you purchase a starter kit. This "instant infrastructure" helps to eliminate many of the stumbling blocks you face when you build your own business from scratch.

- **Variety of selling opportunities.** Gone are the days when direct selling was limited to working for Avon or Tupperware. Today you can represent companies that sell all types of products and wares, ranging from spa products to wine, gourmet food, or clothing. It's a large and diverse industry that boasts nearly $30 billion per year in US sales.

- **Flexibility.** You can exercise complete control over where, when, and how you work (the majority of direct sellers work less than ten hours per week). This is a very portable business that can work wherever you are—an especially nice benefit if you want to travel or take time off for visits with the grandkids.

- **Minimal start-up costs.** You can open a direct sales business for a fraction of what it would cost to start a conventional business. Most direct sales companies charge less than $200 for their initial starter packages.

- **Social benefits.** Entrepreneurs often complain of feeling isolated. But when you work for a direct sales company, you get to be part of a larger team. Many companies host online training sessions and conferences where you can learn, network, exchange ideas, and socialize as part of your job.

- **Income potential.** Most people in direct sales earn less than $3,000 per year, but most people also work their businesses on a very part-time basis. If you are willing to invest the effort, you can turn this into a more serious part- or full-time income stream. In addition to sales commissions, some companies offer miscellaneous incentives, such as free trips or gift certificates as bonuses for high performers. If your company has a multilevel marketing compensation plan, you could also receive payment for recruiting other sellers into the organization (and earn a commission off a percentage of their sales as well).

Like any career in sales, the direct sales option is best for people who are relatively outgoing. It is not the best choice if you are shy or uncomfortable with the thought of asking your friends or relatives to purchase your products. Unfortunately this is also an industry that has been plagued by scams, pyramid schemes, and less-than-ethical operators, so please don't be fooled by promises of "instant riches" or let yourself be pressured into buying large amounts of product that might be difficult to unload. Remember, if it sounds too good to be true, it probably is. It takes consistent effort and commitment to build up a direct sales income, just as it does in any other type of business. Do your homework, find a company you like, make sure both the products and the company are legitimate, and choose a compensation plan that rewards you fairly and generously for your efforts. As this next profile illustrates, if you put the effort into finding the right company, a career in direct sales can provide a welcome combination of flexibility, personal fulfillment, and income during your semi-retirement years.

From Nurse to Direct Sales Superstar

"I look for someone who has confidence and who conveys to me that they want to be successful."
—Karen Pagliurolo, regional manager and sales consultant
    for Etcetera

Growing up, Karen Pagliurolo always enjoyed fashion, but she never expected that one day she would get to make a living from working in the fashion industry. A registered nurse by training, she became a stay-at-home mom in order to accommodate the demands of her husband's career as a major league baseball player. During her early parenting years, she kept busy raising children, running the household, and doing a "ton" of volunteering. But when she received a phone call from a recruiter for the women's clothing company Etcetera, asking if she would be interested in working with them as a home-based direct sales consultant, Karen, then age forty-one, decided she was ready for a new challenge.

Etcetera (www.etcetera.com) is a high-end direct sales fashion company that sells chic everyday clothing via appointment-only trunk shows. Karen paid a small fee to get started with Etcetera, which she quickly recouped with the sales from her first show, and under the tutelage of her area sales manager, a Harvard MBA, she soon built up a loyal following of clients. Karen hosts trunk shows four times a year in the basement of her home in Winchester, Massachusetts, where her clients get to enjoy a personal shopping experience that is a welcome change from the hassles of shopping at department stores. She is paid a commission on all her sales, and in addition receives steep discounts on Etcetera's clothing. Although her life is admittedly hectic during the weeks leading up to and immediately following the shows, this is a business that allows Karen to have considerable flexibility during most of the year. In fact, for several years she successfully balanced her Etcetera business with a second home-based job as a recruiter for a healthcare company.

In 2011, she was promoted to a position as a regional sales manager, helping to recruit and train new consultants. Karen actively recruits women of all ages, but believes that the job of independent sales consultant is an especially good fit for older women. "In fact," Karen says, "I think women in their fifties are probably the best candidates I see. They are educated, they've been active volunteers, and they are the CEOs of their households."

Working as an independent sales consultant has enriched Karen's life in a myriad of unexpected ways; it allows her to control her own destiny and earn a good income, while having fun and flexibility on the job. The benefits of being affiliated with a larger company are not lost on Karen. "It allows me to work on my terms and yet I have the support of my manager to help me grow as a person," says Karen. "I get compensated well and feel like I am part of something bigger." That blend of teamwork and independence proved to be a winning formula for Karen, and now, as a regional manager, she helps empower other women to enjoy the same success, fulfillment, and satisfaction in their own home-based businesses.

Karen's Top Three Tips for Direct Sales Success

1. **Pick a company with a strong management team.** Karen says she has felt supported by management at Etcetera during every step of her professional career. Her first manager was an inspirational role model whose training and support were invaluable to Karen's development and success.

2. **Value your volunteer and life skills (even if you never got paid for them).** Women are rarely given enough credit for all their

accomplishments. If you are motivated and organized and have strong networking skills, you can be very successful at this type of business.

3. **Do work only if it is personally satisfying.** Karen has always viewed her job with Etcetera as being about more than just selling clothes. She derives great satisfaction from helping her customers look and feel terrific, and she is passionate about empowering her consultants to be successful businesswomen in their own right.

To learn more: The Direct Selling Association (www.dsa.org) is the single best resource on the Web for learning about direct selling (including the differences between direct sales and multilevel marketing companies) and for finding links to approved direct sales companies.

FRANCHISES

If the word "franchise" brings to mind businesses like Dunkin' Donuts and Starbucks, it's time to update your thinking. The world of franchising has expanded way beyond fast-food chains and retail stores to include smaller service businesses that can be run on a flexible schedule. Franchises are a potentially attractive semi-retirement option for several reasons:

- Franchises boast a lower failure rate than businesses started from scratch; consequently loans are generally easier to obtain for these types of businesses.

- As a franchisee, you can take advantage of a recognized brand and a tested business plan, which can ease the risks associated with being out on your own.

- Franchises provide ongoing marketing, training, and other support to help keep your business running smoothly.

Of course, there are also considerable risks and challenges associated with the franchising model. This is typically the most costly business-in-a-box alternative. Even part-time and small franchises can be expensive to purchase, and in addition to the normal costs of doing business, there are licensing requirements, long-term obligations, and ongoing royalty fees that may be required. As a franchisee, you compromise your ability to fully control your business. Not only must you follow the franchisor's policies and procedures, but your success is tied to their performance; if the company enjoys great press, you benefit, and if they are embroiled in a scandal or file for bankruptcy, you will be negatively impacted as well.

It goes without saying that the decision to open a franchise should not be taken lightly; it requires careful thought, planning, and evaluation of the risks. Take the time to clarify your personal objectives, lifestyle goals, and willingness to accept financial risk before starting your franchise search. If work-life flexibility is paramount, avoid brick-and-mortar franchises. Be prepared to spend time on research, ask tough questions, talk to other franchisees, and meet with an attorney and accountant prior to entering into any franchise agreement.

Franchises can work well for both novice and seasoned entrepreneurs. As you'll learn in this next story, the benefits of having access to an instant infrastructure and proven business methodology can offer a very attractive combination for people who want to avoid the headaches typically associated with independent start-up ventures.

From Solopreneur to Franchisee

"Do your homework, do your homework, do your homework."
—Kathy McShane, Ladies Who Launch Franchisee
   of Southwestern Connecticut

For eighteen years, Kathy McShane, age sixty, of New Canaan, Connecticut, ran a highly successful multimillion-dollar promotions company. But after the business hit tough times in 2008, Kathy decided it was time to close the agency and shift gears. She returned to school and earned both a certification in coaching from NYU and a certification in positive psychology from the University of Pennsylvania, with plans to teach positive psychology as part of her next career. Around that time, a friend introduced her to the business incubator groups run by Ladies Who Launch, a company that helps women entrepreneurs build their new business ventures. Even though she already had significant experience as an entrepreneur, Kathy decided to sign up for the incubator sessions—and quickly fell in love with the program's methodology and protocol.

From the beginning of her second-act journey, Kathy's objective was very clear: she wanted to help women build and grow successful businesses. But she was reluctant to go through the laborious process of building a new business from the ground up again. "That is why I found the business-in-a-box model so attractive," says Kathy. "It helped simplify the start-up process." After consulting with an attorney, she purchased a Ladies Who Launch franchise for $15,000. "The technology and the training alone were worth the cost of the entry," remarks Kathy. In addition to the initial payment, Kathy pays the franchise a percentage of the fees she charges for the different events she offers. "I don't mind it," she says, pointing out that the fees help to pay for things like website costs that she would pay for as a normal part of doing business.

Although Kathy was confident about the franchise idea from the start, she admits that her husband and friends expressed concern that she would feel encumbered by the franchise's rules and restrictions. Although not everything has always worked perfectly, Kathy maintains that the franchise route has proven to be a good fit for her needs. That said, there are some things she would do differently if she were going through the selection process again.

Kathy's Top Three Tips for Franchisees

1. **Remain objective.** Try not to fall in love with one franchise; even if you think you've found the perfect fit, take your time and look at other options. It is always helpful to research your full range of possibilities thoroughly before purchasing a franchise.

2. **Ask a lot of questions.** Develop a questionnaire ahead of time and get answers to every question you have on the list.

3. **Know what you are buying.** Talk with other people who already own the same franchise to solicit their views and input. Drill down far enough to ensure that you get to know the management team, their commitment to people in the field, and their marketing plans. Don't hesitate to use social media and other networking tools to better understand what specifically you are buying for your dollars.

To learn more about franchise opportunities, look into these resources:

- *Entrepreneur* magazine offers a wealth of information about franchises through their website, books, and magazine at www .entrepreneur.com. You'll find lists of franchises including "10 Franchises for $20K (or Less)" and "The Best Home-Based Franchises," which include franchises that can be purchased for less than a $5,000 initial investment.

- International Franchise Association (www.franchise.org) is the world's oldest and largest organization representing franchising worldwide.

LICENSEE

Successful service professionals (coaches, consultants, speakers) sometimes package their proven systems into off-the-shelf programs that they sell to colleagues for use in their own practices. In addition to offering content and materials, they train you on their systems and grant you a license to deliver their turnkey programs to your clients.

To better understand how this works in real life, let's take a look at the train-the-trainer business etiquette programs offered by the Emily Post Institute (www.emilypost.com). Imagine that you are an independent consultant who has noticed a need among your clients for coaching on business etiquette. You could spend months developing and testing your own programs, or you could invest in a one-week class with the Emily Post Institute and quickly leverage their years of experience and brand name recognition into a training program of your own. Upon completing the course and paying a small licensing fee, you have the right to use their training materials (PowerPoint slides, worksheets, and so on) and can promote yourself as having trained with the Institute and use their "Trained by Emily Post" seal on your website. Graduates of their programs are also entitled to additional coaching with the staff at the Post Institute and can purchase their etiquette books at a steep discount for use in their own workshops.

I've taken advantage of these off-the-shelf programs in my own coaching practice and found them to be an efficient way to expand my offerings without having to invest energy in developing my own content. It has saved me money and time (and angst) that I can apply to other parts of my business. In my case, I decided to become a licensed facilitator of Laura Berman Fortgang's Now What? coaching program, a twelve-week system that provides my clients with an alternative to my regular à la carte coaching services. To qualify as a facilitator, I paid a one-time fee, attended a training course, and passed a final exam. As a certified facilitator, not only do I have the right to use the Now What? program and materials in my own practice, but I also get to take advantage of special facilitator-only conference calls, newsletters, and follow-up trainings that Laura provides at no additional cost.

How do you learn about these types of packages in your own industry? Conferences, industry meetings, and associations can be good places to discover these opportunities within your own industry (the vendor areas are often rich with industry experts selling their programs). The terms, benefits, and fees involved with being a licensed facilitator vary from provider to provider, so be sure to shop around, check references, and compare your options before investing your time or money.

BUY A BUSINESS STARTER KIT

Have you ever read about a business and thought, "That sounds like a cool idea!" but you lacked the know-how to turn your interest into action? Next time you have one of those "hmmm . . ." moments, do some research to see whether you can find a business starter kit that you can use as a blueprint. Starter kits are typically created by people who have years of experience running their businesses; they include the step-by-step instructions, templates, forms, and other resources that you need to get your own business launched. More expensive starter kits might also provide one-to-one consulting services, access to specialized databases, and/or website hosting services. These kits can save you considerable time, money, and aggravation. But like other forms of unregulated training (certification programs, webinars, and so on), the value and practicality of these kits varies tremendously, so once again, be sure to do your homework before investing your money.

Purchasing a high quality starter kit can be an economical alternative to the pricier and more restrictive franchise model. Take a look at this next story to learn how one California woman used a starter kit as a way to launch a successful home-based business.

Profile of a Starter Kit Success Story

"There are so many scams on the Internet and you cannot be too careful."
—Penny Spark, owner of Southern California Home
   Improvement Referral Service

It's funny how sometimes our best business ideas happen when we least expect them. Penny Spark's lightbulb moment came as a result of the frustrations she experienced while renovating her home. After spending months dealing with unreliable contractors and wanting "to tear my hair out," Penny read an article about the Homeowners Referral Network (HRN), a service that helps people find reliable home contractors. The article mentioned that HRN sold business starter packages for people interested in starting their own referral businesses. Penny was instantly intrigued by the HRN concept, especially because she had recently sold her old business and was actively looking for her next venture. She called the company, asked for information, and ran the numbers. Then after reviewing the business model, she called the founder of HRN, Debra Cohen, and "bombarded" her with questions. "I really put the poor woman through the wringer," recalls Penny with a laugh.

It was time well spent; the more they talked, the more comfortable Penny felt. The fact that HRN was *not* a franchise was a big plus for Penny, who worried that the restrictions associated with the franchise model could be suffocating. "I am an entrepreneur, and I needed to be free to take my ideas and run with them," she says. After careful consideration, Penny purchased the HRN manual, along with eight hours of one-to-one consulting time with Debra, and barely two months later she opened for business. Today her concierge-style service (based out of her home in Sierra Madre, California) helps clients find contractors for their commercial, residential, and industrial projects.

Thirteen years after purchasing a manual and consulting services that enabled her to open a business in an arena where she had little prior experience, Penny, now age fifty-five, is certain that she made a wise choice by choosing to work with both Debra and HRN. "Debra understands that making the sale is only the first step," says Penny. "She knew my success would be her success. And here we both are, thirteen years later."

Penny's Top Three Tips for Entrepreneurs

1. **Find a business that suits your lifestyle.** It's not easy to balance starting a business and running a business. For some people the franchise model is ideal—it can teach you what you need to do every step of the way. For others, it is too restrictive. Know what is right for you.

2. **Ask for references.** You have to make sure not only that what you are buying is a viable business, but that the person you're buying from is ethical and telling you the truth. Call other licensees, ask lots of questions, and don't hesitate to ask for multiple references.

3. **Invest time in building relationships.** Penny's business operates on a small budget, so she relies on business networking, repeat business, referrals, and the Internet to secure her clients.

For more information: Industry magazines and trade associations can be good resources for locating information about starter kits. If you aren't ready to invest in a full-service kit, you might want to purchase a less expensive business starter guide or manual. Two websites, Fabjob.com and Entrepreneur.com, sell basic starter guides covering a wide variety of entrepreneurial businesses.

SELL ON eBAY (AND OTHER ONLINE MARKETPLACES)

The Internet has simplified the process of turning your trash into treasures and collectibles into cash. And while most people use online marketplace sites primarily to earn just a little extra cash, if you take the time to learn how to buy, sell, and market smartly, you can actually earn real money—sometimes even the equivalent of a modest full-time income—selling goods online. The economic impact of eBay is enormous: in 2011, the total value of goods sold on eBay was $68.6 billion—more than $2,100 *every second*. It is the world's largest online marketplace, where people around the globe can buy and sell practically anything including cookie jars, antique paintings, or a bag full of children's socks. Although it is the biggest online marketplace, eBay is not the only player in this space, and there are many other online marketplaces where you can potentially sell your goods. Here are three of the bigger sites:

- **Bonanza.com.** A rising star in the online marketplace galaxy, Bonanza specializes in items that you can't find mass-produced in stores, like purses, vintage clothing, antiques, jewelry, memorabilia, and collectibles. Their tagline, "Everything but the ordinary," sums it up well.

- **Etsy.com.** Etsy is the online marketplace for handmade items and crafts, including art, furniture, glass, clothing, candles, and more. Etsy has a very vibrant online community where you can exchange ideas, access online training and learn about educational and networking events.

- **Amazon.com.** Merchants can sell a wide variety of products and inventory on Amazon.com. You can download a guide from their site that explains how to get started selling as a merchant on Amazon.

Earning a living as an online merchant is not unlike every other business; if you want to succeed, you need to learn the rules of the road, be realistic about your expectations, and be willing to adapt when necessary. As you'll learn from the tips offered in this next profile, success selling online is more about being a savvy businessperson than it is about just being a smart shopper.

From Disabled Executive to eBay Hall of Fame

"I had no interest in collectibles—my interest was in being busy and productive."
—"Uncle" Joe Adamson, eBay Hall of Fame

Joe Adamson was a technology executive in his thirties when he became seriously ill—so ill that his doctor told him that it was unlikely that he could ever return to work. Overnight Joe went from climbing the corporate ladder to staring at the television for hours on end. "I watched my brain cells marching out the door," recalls Joe. "I was no longer useful. I was no longer desirable. I was no longer needed. If they had rolled tanks up in front of my house, it couldn't have been any worse. It was quite a shock." As the months wore on and Joe began to acclimate to his new normal, he focused on the difficult process of pulling his life together and moving forward.

Fortunately he was familiar with the online world, and because he had friends who owned a local surplus store, he decided to try his hand selling their secondhand items on eBay, figuring it would be a relatively easy way to supplement his income. He began by selling rosin animal head statues, collector pocketknives, tools, and other items that he could physically handle. He figured out the best ways to market the items online, and with time, he started to increase sales.

Joe acknowledges that his background was tailor-made for online success: he has strong communication skills, he had designed IT networks, and he knows how to sell, how to write, how to take pictures, and how to make videos. As he notes on his website, "It's been said that I was raised in a laboratory, created in a petri dish, with e-commerce skills gene-spliced into my DNA." With that winning combination of personality, determination, and skills, it wasn't long before Joe's business flourished. "I got really good at it, really fast," says Joe. "I was in the right place, at the right time, with the right mix of products."

Today Joe still sells on eBay, but his main income now comes from teaching and mentoring other people interested in learning how to create their own eBay success. He is a certified eBay education specialist who shares his expertise through his training programs, meet-up groups, and the informational offerings on his website at www.unclejoeradio.com. Joe also helps to run the eBay meet-up group where he lives in Oklahoma City, Oklahoma.

His work these days is as much about giving back as it is about earning his own livelihood. Joe knows all too well what it feels like to be down on your luck. He frequently offers his time to people in need, but they in turn must be willing to make the effort to change. "It is my one-man mission to help fight unnecessary poverty," shares Joe. "I know that some of the people I work with are fifty bucks away from having their lights turned off." Helping these people learn how to sell on eBay starts them on a path that enables them to be productive and valued and to have a sense of worth. Joe believes that if he can impart that knowledge to people, he can imbue them with the skills to "go out there and get it done" and, in the process, help to turn their lives around.

Joe's Top Six Tips for eBay Selling Success

1. **It's more about the selling than the buying.** People have a great time shopping and treasure hunting. It can be wonderful fun. But at some point, you need to do the work and sell. "Selling" doesn't just mean posting items online; you need to write compelling content, post attractive photos, and be realistic and competitive about pricing.

2. **Remember the Golden Rule.** eBay operates on a rating system, and bad feedback is ruinous for sellers. The sellers who go above and beyond in their customer service tend to be very successful. They always pay attention to detail and have a dogged determination to be "white-glove honest."

3. **Be a smart shopper.** The two ways to make money on eBay are by buying right and by buying with efficiency. It takes as much effort to sell something for a fifty-dollar profit as it does to make a five-dollar profit, so it's important to concentrate your buying on items that have the best markup potential. Don't allow yourself to become emotionally connected to your purchases.

4. **Invest in education.** eBay.com offers online training that takes people through all the steps necessary to start selling on eBay. Once you know the basics, it can be very helpful to learn more from certified training specialists. Certified specialists, like Joe, have been teaching for some time and generally have their own successful businesses. Specialists can also provide ongoing mentoring for people who want to take their business to the next level.

5. **Participate in the eBay community.** This is a warm group of people with a helpful spirit. There are numerous online spaces where people exchange shoptalk, resources, and tips. As Joe says, "We don't have a union hall or meeting place, so we meet online." There are also groups that meet in person (you can locate them on www.meetup.com), discussion boards, and groups you can find listed under the community tab on eBay and on Facebook. eBay hosts several "on location" seminars and conferences that are terrific events for networking and learning; people who pay to attend these conferences tend to be a good group of people to know, because they are either already very successful or "up-and-comers" in the business.

6. **Don't trust everything you read online.** New sellers should be aware that the online groups and message boards can sometimes be simmering kettles of negativity. You need to interpret their comments carefully and remember that people generally don't go online to celebrate—they go online to kvetch, vent, and let off steam.

The growth of online marketplaces has created a whole new industry designed to support, educate, and unite people involved in this profession. To learn more, start with a basic Google search; you'll find conferences, meet-up groups, online forums, training programs, and books to help you succeed and thrive in this world.

- Two books of note are *Starting an eBay Business for Dummies* by Marsha Collier (For Dummies, 2011) and *The Handmade Marketplace: How to Sell Your Crafts Locally, Globally, and Online* by Kari Chapin (Storey Publishing, 2010).

- eBay offers a helpful learning center at http://pages.ebay.com /education/index.html.

THREE FINAL TIPS FOR PEOPLE INTERESTED IN PURSUING A BUSINESS-IN-A-BOX OPPORTUNITY

1. **Do your homework.** You've read this advice several times already, but it bears repeating. There are many questionable opportunities out there, and you can't be too careful. Ask lots of questions, call other people who are involved with the business, and, when needed, consult with an attorney or accountant before investing money.

2. **Beware of scams.** Here are some of the warning signs to look for:

   - The ad uses phrases like "No experience needed," "Unlimited earning potential," or "Make hundreds a week."

   - The ad is vague, and job responsibilities are not clearly defined. No company address is listed.

{continued}

- For a fee, the business will send you a list of companies interested in home-based workers or a kit of products to assemble.

    If your gut tells you something is amiss, pay attention to it. Don't hesitate to check out your suspicions by calling the Better Business Bureau (in the state where the company is based) to check for complaints filed against the company. You can also contact the attorney general's office in your state or the state where the company is located. A well-placed phone call may save you considerable aggravation and money.

3. **Decide whether you're comfortable with having to "color inside the lines"—whether you're a leader or a follower.** Business-in-a-box models take a lot of the guesswork out of creating a business, but for some people, the restrictions and formulas are suffocating. Find a model that works with *your* goals and *your* personality. If you want something that you can shape, mold, and tailor from scratch, you will probably be better off striking out on your own.

CHAPTER FIVE

Trade Your Time for a Paycheck

Up until now, we have been exploring entrepreneurial options. But not everyone is eager to start their own business. Some people are far more comfortable with the structure, camaraderie, and support offered by being employed by, or associated with, a larger entity. If you think you might prefer to find a job, or work on a freelance or project basis, then this is the chapter for you. In this section, we will examine different ways you can trade your time for a paycheck: either as a part-time or seasonal employee, by securing a freelance assignment, or as a temporary worker affiliated with a temporary agency or interim executive services firm. Let's begin by discussing the traditional option of part-time jobs.

PART-TIME JOBS

If I had a dollar for every person who came into my office and said, "I'd love a job, but I really only want to work part-time," I'd be a wealthy woman. I understand that desire. Part-time work is attractive; it offers the familiarity of a set schedule, a predictable paycheck, and the support provided by a traditional work setting, all without the demands of a full-time job. Some part-time jobs, like working at a neighborhood bookstore or at the local library, can be an especially pleasant alternative for people in semi-retirement. And it is not just "easy" jobs that are now being done on a part-time basis; quality part-time professional jobs are on the rise as more employers are increasingly willing to consider creative alternatives to full-time schedules.

Finding those quality part-time openings can still be a challenge though, and if working as a part-time professional is your goal, you'll need to employ slightly different strategies than you would if searching for a full-time job. But if you are willing to invest the energy, interesting part-time jobs can be found. Here are some of the best tactics for part-time job-search success:

- **Talk to your former employers.** They know your value, and under the right circumstances they may welcome having you back on payroll. Even if they can't give you a regular part-time position, they may be willing to offer you project or temporary work assignments, and over time those assignments could lead to a more permanent arrangement. (One note of caution: retirees who work for the same employer from which they retired should check with the benefits department to see whether their reemployment status will affect their pension benefits.)

- **Target small businesses.** My clients are most successful at finding part-time jobs when they target small businesses and entrepreneurial firms. Why? Many small-business owners have learned that by offering flexibility they can attract and retain top-level talent who might not work for them otherwise. Small-business owners also appreciate the value offered by part-time workers who often prove to be as productive as their more costly full-time counterparts. Of course, not every small business is a good fit for this; companies that operate under tight deadlines or are heavily involved in client services will not be as accommodating as companies where the work can be completed on a more flexible timetable.

- **Explore opportunities with entrepreneurs.** Working for a successful entrepreneur offers several of the advantages of being in your own business—flexible hours, work-from-home options, and varied job responsibilities—with none of the risks associated with running your own show. If you want to find opportunities working with entrepreneurs, plan to attend meetings of small-business groups, such as your local chamber of commerce, to increase your network of entrepreneurial contacts. Venture capital (VC) firms can also be a good source of leads about part-time openings with start-up companies. Check with colleagues for recommendations of VCs (this can be a clubby world, so it helps to network your way into a conversation). Gust.com is a good site for information about angel investors and VC firms.

- **Consider local cultural, religious, and community-based institutions.** Museums, theaters, arts agencies, churches, temples, and libraries all rely heavily on part-time workers to meet their staffing needs. Although the compensation packages at these institutions are not as rich as those offered by corporate employers, their social, cultural, and educational benefits and perks can be very appealing.

THE POWER TRIO OF FLEXIBILITY: EDUCATION, HEALTHCARE, AND SALES

Part-time and flexible jobs have long been a staple in education, healthcare, and sales-related occupations. Here is some helpful background on each of these three industries:

Education

Teaching can be an appealing option for midlife career changers who want an opportunity to share their knowledge and make a difference in the lives of future generations. According to the 2012–13 online version of the *Occupational Outlook Handbook*, the hiring outlook for teachers is looking strong for the foreseeable future, although hiring conditions are, of course, impacted by budgets, legislation, and the general health of the economy. Employment prospects for teachers tend to be better in inner cities and rural areas than in suburban districts, and are expected to be strongest for math, science, bilingual, and special education teachers.

Attaining a teaching certification has become easier in recent years, with nearly all fifty states offering some form of alternative teaching certification for people who have either a bachelor's degree or significant work experience in the subject they will teach, but who lack the educational courses needed for credentialing. The cost of training may run from a few thousand dollars to more than $15,000, but you might be able to reduce those costs if you qualify for grants or loan forgiveness programs. Former military personnel who want to retrain as teachers may qualify for financial assistance and counseling through the Troops to Teachers program (www.proudtoserveagain.com). Teachers in private schools do not have to be licensed but typically still need a bachelor's degree to be considered for employment (and some private schools will expect you to become certified within a year or so after employment).

Life as a teacher is both rewarding and challenging. And although you will get to enjoy having summers off and plentiful school holidays and break periods, the day-to-day demands of the classroom can be considerable, especially for new teachers. One of the best ways to determine if you'll enjoy life in the classroom is to test it out as a substitute teacher (contact your local school system for details on how to apply as a sub). Alternatively, you could volunteer to work in the classroom, but if you do, remember that teaching in a suburban elementary school will likely be a very different experience from teaching in an urban high school, so be sure to give preference to volunteer settings that match your longer-term career objectives.

To learn more about teaching careers:

- Look into alternative certification programs from the National Center for Alternative Certification (www.teach-now.org).

- Find information on loan forgiveness programs from the American Federation of Teachers at www.aft.org/yourwork/tools4teachers/fundingdatabase.

- Consult your local colleges to find out about their teacher training programs.

Healthcare

Healthcare employment opportunities are expanding, and as baby boomers grow older and live longer, the demand for healthcare workers should continue to be exceptionally strong. According to the US Bureau of Labor Statistics, approximately 26 percent of all new jobs created between 2008 and 2018 will be in the healthcare and social assistance industries. Healthcare careers are an excellent option for semi-retired people looking for meaningful work outside the corporate box. It is an industry in which maturity is valued and opportunities for flexible scheduling are robust. A career in healthcare usually requires some type of certification or training, although the majority of jobs require less than a four-year degree. Here are some options to explore if you want to pursue a part-time or flexible healthcare career:

- **Holistic/alternative practitioner.** There is a growing acceptance of holistic healing alternatives including hypnosis, reflexology, acupuncture, and naturopathy—even within the traditional world of mainstream medicine. Although you could be employed by a hospital, most practitioners in these disciplines usually work independently or affiliate with small private practices. To find more information about careers in holistic medicine, consult www.alternativemedicine.net.

- **Diet and nutrition counselor.** The obesity epidemic is driving a growing need for professionals who can provide nutritional counseling, behavioral therapies, and exercise advice to help people gain better control over their weight. If you're interested in this field but don't want to go back to school for an advanced degree, you may want to explore a career as a health coach. The Institute for Integrative Nutrition has a one-year training program (www .integrativenutrition.com), run in partnership with the State University of New York at Purchase College, for people interested in becoming health and nutrition coaches.

- **Fitness instructors.** The boomer generation grew up with Jane Fonda, aerobics, and Jazzercise. But as they age, they will be looking for fitness teachers who can help them stay in shape without placing undue stress on their aging bodies, joint replacements, or fragile bones. As a fitness instructor, you can work at senior centers, gyms, and in private homes. To learn more about becoming a fitness professional, consult the American Council on Exercise at www.acefitness.org. For information about Pilates certification, contact the Pilates Method Alliance at www .pilatesmethodalliance.org; for information about yoga training, check with the Yoga Alliance at yogaalliance.org.

- **Physical therapist aide or assistant.** Physical therapist aides and assistants help physical therapists provide therapeutic services to their patients. This field offers many good opportunities for part-time and flexible working hours. According to the *Occupational Outlook Handbook*, 72 percent of physical therapy employees work in offices of other health practitioners and in hospitals; the remainder work in nursing care facilities, home healthcare services, and outpatient care centers. For more information, consult the American Physical Therapy Association at www.apta.org.

- **Medical assistants.** Medical assistants perform medical and clerical tasks that help keep the offices of a doctor or healthcare practitioner running smoothly. Formal training in medical assisting is not required, but there are one-year certificate and two-year associate programs for those wishing to get advanced training. For more information, consult the American Association of Medical Assistants at www.aama-ntl.org or consult your community college catalog for their class listings.

- **Phlebotomy technician specialist.** Phlebotomists help to draw and collect blood samples. Upon successful completion of forty-five hours of classroom instruction and an additional thirty hours of hands-on phlebotomy training, students are eligible to take an examination offered by the National Health Career Association (www.nhanow.com) to become a certified phlebotomist.

- **EKG technician.** Trained EKG technicians run the heart monitoring equipment in cardiologist offices, rehabilitation programs, and hospital cardiac catheterization laboratories. Training typically consists of approximately twenty hours of classroom instruction and an additional twenty-plus hours of hands-on training. Students who successfully complete the training are eligible to take an exam administered by the National Health Career Association for certification.

- **Dental assistant.** Dental assistants educate patients on dental care, take X-rays, and perform other functions in a dental office. Many assistants learn their skills on the job, although an increasing number are trained in dental-assisting programs that take one year or less to complete. For more information, consult the American Dental Assistants Association at www.dentalassistant.org.

Sales

Talented salespeople are always in demand. During weak economic times, strong salespeople keep companies afloat, and during prosperous times they help companies tap into new markets and increase profit margins. Compensation for sales jobs is directly linked to performance, and results matter far more than how, when, or where you spend your time. If you meet or exceed your goals, you'll be rewarded, even if your "face time" is not as high as that of your full-time colleagues. As a result, top salespeople can earn impressive incomes, irrespective of the number of hours they work. This is in sharp contrast to many other lifestyle-friendly jobs, for which flexible schedules all too often result in reduced earning potential.

Real estate sales is one of the more popular options for semi-retirees, and if you enjoy working in sales and live in an area with a strong real estate market, it can be a good second-act career. But as any successful real estate agent will attest, life as a real estate agent isn't quite as flexible as some think; although you can work as much or as little as you want (within reason), successful agents tend to work quite hard, and you should expect to work some evenings and weekends. This is also an industry that has been negatively impacted by both the Internet and the sluggish housing market, so be sure to research the outlook for real estate agents in your local area before you invest in training. Real estate brokers and sales agents must be licensed and people who want to earn a broker's license need both formal training and experience selling real estate, usually one to three years. To learn more, consult the National Association of Realtors at www.realtor.org.

JOBS "WITH BENEFITS"

A surprising number of part-time jobs include special benefits, perks, and unique experiences that could add extra incentive to your official compensation package. Here are some of the benefits that might be included as part of your job:

- Crazy about travel? Careers in the travel industry don't always pay top salaries, but the perks are priceless. Employees of travel-related companies like airlines, hotels, travel agencies, and cruise ships can enjoy significant travel discounts. In some situations, they may also be entitled to discounts from affiliated travel providers (for example, an employee with a cruise ship might be entitled to discounts at select hotels).

- Love to learn? Employees of colleges and universities are often entitled to tuition discounts—a valuable benefit that can apply to family members as well. Even if you have no interest in earning another degree (or if your college's tuition benefits don't extend to part-timers), working on a college campus gives you easy access to symposiums, lectures, book readings, and special exhibits. On larger campuses, you may also be entitled to free use of the university gym or complimentary tickets to college sporting events.

- Fan of fashion? Department stores and clothing manufacturers normally give their employees a significant discount on their in-house purchases. Some employers also invite their employees to special trunk shows, sample sales, and end-of-the-season clearance events, where they can buy clothing and accessories at a steep savings.

- Are you a sports fan? If spending a day at a sporting event is your idea of sheer bliss, consider working for a company that is connected to the sports industry. Jobs with a sports-related venue, media company, professional association, or team can give you access to free or discounted tickets to major sporting events. You don't need to be an athlete to get hired in this industry; there are opportunities for people with sales, public relations, management, human resources, financial, and accounting skills.

Remember that these little perks can add up and make a real difference in both your compensation package and the fun factor associated with your job.

You never know where, when, or how you might find that perfect part-time job. As this next story illustrates, sometimes the best opportunities surface when you least expect them.

From Retired to Rehired: A VP with Flex Hours

"It's very refreshing to not worry about climbing the ladder after doing that for so many years."
—Joanne Schumacher, VP with flex hours

After enjoying a long career in recruiting and staffing management for high-tech firms in Silicon Valley, California, Joanne Schumacher and her husband looked forward to a retirement filled with leisure and travel. They moved to a retirement community in Northern California and quickly settled into a routine filled with golf, social outings, and community activities. All went according to plan, until one morning while browsing an e-mail newsletter, Joanne read about a job with a start-up called Staffingbook, an online service that connects third-party recruiters representing passive candidates to employers. Although she wasn't actively looking for work, Joanne was so intrigued by the job description that on a whim she decided to apply.

From her first conversation with the company's owner, Joanne knew she had found a good fit. "The owner is an expert at building companies, I am an expert in recruiting, and the third employee is an expert in building software," Joanne said. "We all complement each other—it is just a really nice combination of skills." Although she was officially hired as the vice president in charge of subscriber services, like most employees in small start-up situations, Joanne wears many hats and juggles a variety of tasks each day. Nonetheless, she finds the fast pace of the job exhilarating. "I thrive on change," she says. Given that it is a start-up situation, she works for a "very modest salary" that is significantly lower than her old compensation as a recruiter, but she holds an equity stake in the company that she hopes will prove lucrative in the not-too-distant future.

Joanne spends about thirty hours a week on the job. Most days she commutes to the office, but she can work from home when it is convenient to do so. Her schedule leaves her with "enough" time to enjoy life in her retirement community, albeit not as many hours as she originally planned. It is an arrangement that seems to work for both Joanne and her husband, who has been retired for several years. "I thought maybe I'd resent working knowing he is home, but I don't," observes Joanne. "I love working, and I think it is healthy for each of us to have our own time to do what we want to do."

How long she will remain working depends on the success of Staffingbook, her health, and her desire to continue with the job. Noting that her own parents worked well into their seventies, Joanne, now sixty-seven, anticipates working for many years to come. But in the meantime, she is enjoying the chance to build a new company without feeling the pressures she would have when she was just starting out in her career. Looking back on her unexpected second-act career, she is still amazed at how easily things fell into place. "I guess sometimes I say I believe in fate," Joanne observes. "When it is the right thing, it just works well."

Joanne's Top Three Tips for Working Part-Time in Retirement

1. **Keep an open mind.** You never know what type of job might prove to be a great fit, so be open to new ideas and new ways of working.

2. **Do something you enjoy.** Life is too short to make sacrifices. Remember, you aren't climbing the corporate ladder anymore.

3. **Don't be afraid to negotiate.** What do you have to lose? Ask for what you want, and you just might get it—more flexible hours, time off for travel and volunteering, work-from-home options, company equity instead of salary, and so on.

ADVICE FROM THE FLEXJOBS EXPERT

"Have hope! There are many more professional part-time and flexible jobs available than you might expect."
—SARA FELL, CEO and founder, FlexJobs.com

Sara Fell manages a job board that specializes in flexible job listings. Her team of trained researchers has found flexible jobs in virtually all industries and at all levels, including managerial and executive roles. Here is a sampling of recent professional part-time jobs listed at www.flexjobs.com:

- Ombudsman
- Chief financial officer
- Aquarist/Zookeeper
- Senior systems engineer
- Master schedule consultant
- Website Coeditor and writer for a chronic pain website
- Associate professor, Child Studies
- Psychologist
- Associate general counsel
- Executive director

The jobs on FlexJobs.com offer a range of flexible benefits, including telecommuting, flexible schedules, and alternative schedules. Sara cautions that you should be aware that there are often degrees of flexibility with these work options—a job might offer telecommuting three days a week but not every day, or a flexible schedule but one that is not completely in your control.

Sara also warns that professional part-time and flexible jobs can be difficult to find among the piles of less-skilled jobs, ads, and scams. A keyword search for "part-time jobs" will generally yield an abundance of retail, restaurant, and student jobs, but fewer higher-level positions. Similarly, if you're interested in finding a job that allows you to work from home, you'll likely find yourself neck-deep in a pile of too-good-to-be-true business opportunities and suspicious-sounding ads.

Sara's Top Three Keyword Search Terms

1. **Part-time jobs:** Be specific, and use "part-time" plus the job title and location you're looking for, such as "part-time engineer in Colorado."

2. **Work-from-home jobs:** Try using "telecommute," "telecommuting," or "remote job" paired with related career words, such as "telecommute marketing jobs." Stay away from "work from home" or "work at home."

3. **Consulting jobs:** It's fine to use "consulting," and be sure to try the variation "consultant" as well as search terms such as "freelance" and "contract" plus your industry.

How to Find Part-Time Job Openings

Now that you know the types of industries and situations most likely to have part-time jobs, the next challenge is figuring out how to find those elusive opportunities:

- **Network, network, network.** As in any job search, the best way to find part-time opportunities is through a process of active networking. Tell everyone you know that you are interested in working part-time; reach out to former colleagues, employers, and personal friends through both in-person initiatives and social media channels.

- **Approach companies directly.** If you don't have a way to network into a company, contact the hiring manager in the department where you would like to work and pitch your part-time services as a solution to their business challenge. For example, if you want to work as a part-time employment interviewer, analyze the classifieds to identify employers who are in an active hiring mode and then contact them about your recruiting services.

- **Temp your way into a part-time job.** Companies like to offer jobs to people who have worked for them on a temporary basis (and it is often easier to sell the company on a part-time schedule if they already know and like you). Some companies maintain a list of on-call temps and others hire contractors through temporary agencies. There are also a growing number of employment services that place people into companies on a flexible basis, such as www.tentiltwo.com, www.flexibleresources.com, and for lawyers, www.flextimelawyers.com.

- **Use the job boards.** Most of the larger online job boards—like Indeed.com, Careerbuilder.com, and SimplyHired.com—provide a filter that allows you to restrict your search results to jobs with flexible or part-time hours. Craigslist.org has become a favorite place for small businesses to post their jobs. You'll find many local positions listed that are difficult to find elsewhere.

- **Look on bulletin boards.** Seriously, you'll be amazed by the number of interesting local listings you'll find advertised on community bulletin boards in libraries, town halls, schools, and recreation centers.

Most important, be patient. Finding a good part-time situation takes perseverance, but the payoff of a less stressful lifestyle, improved flexibility, and a steady part-time paycheck makes it a challenge worth pursuing.

SEASONAL JOBS

Working a seasonal job can be a good solution for people who want to work but don't want to be tied to a job year-round. Although most people equate seasonal work with college students in need of summer jobs, it can also be a good fit for retirees who alternate their time between two residences or who want blocks of time to enjoy their personal interests. That certainly was the case for Penny Frederickson, age fifty-four, from Minneapolis, Minnesota, who sold her daycare center eight years ago and now has two seasonal jobs, one working in sales for a garden center in the summer and a second working for a design firm helping to decorate at Christmastime. "It's lots of fun," she says. "I love plants, I love to garden, I love to decorate, and I get to do all three." The jobs give her a chance to get out of the house, talk to people, and do work she enjoys, while still having plenty of time to travel and relax in between her seasonal jobs.

Here are several examples of seasonal jobs you could pursue:

- **Tax preparation services.** You don't need to be an accountant to prepare tax returns. Large companies like H&R Block offer their own training program for people interested in working for the firm as tax preparers.

- **Summer camps.** Camps hire college students to be counselors, but they also hire more "mature" adults for jobs as camp nurses, cooks, and office workers.

- **Delivery services.** Package delivery services like UPS and FedEx hire extra workers during the peak holiday seasons.

- **Retailers.** Stores hire extra staff to work during the holiday season (and many offer seasonal workers an employee discount—a nice way to offset your holiday shopping expenses).

- **Local government agencies.** Tourist agencies, parks, and recreation departments all need extra assistance during the busy summer and tourist seasons.

The options for working on a seasonal basis are more varied than you may realize. And, as the next expert explains, working a seasonal job could even give you a chance to spend time in some very cool vacation destinations.

ADVICE FROM THE COOLWORKS.COM EXPERT

"Seasonal work is a pretty risk-free way to shake up your life or try something different. You go and do it for a few months. If you don't like it, there is no expectation that you signed on for the long haul."
—BILL BERG, CEO of CoolWorks.com

It was a cold, bleak day in Connecticut when I interviewed Bill Berg, whose website, CoolWorks.com, specializes in "jobs in great places." When I commented on our weather, Bill invited me to take a peek at the webcam on his site so I could enjoy the view outside his office in Gardiner, Montana—an idyllic picture of freshly fallen snow glistening along the Yellowstone River. All it took was one look, and I instantly knew why Bill is so passionate about living and working in our national parks.

Bill first discovered the national parks many years ago when he was a college student looking for a fun job for the summer. A friend suggested that he apply for work in the parks, and Bill ended up spending the summer pumping gas at the service station in Yellowstone. That job turned out to be the first of a series of jobs in the parks for Bill, and he ultimately decided to permanently settle in Yellowstone, where he and his wife have now lived for the better part of their adult lives.

Recognizing that he was not the only one who would love the chance to work in "cool places," Bill created CoolWorks.com in 1995 as an online employment resource for people who want to work seasonal jobs in nice places. The site was originally designed for college students, but it didn't take long before he realized that the site was equally appropriate for the "older and bolder" crowd.

According to Bill, boomers have become an increasingly attractive labor force for summer seasonal employers. "The boomers often come in pairs, bring their own housing (mobile homes), have a wealth of experience, and offer a fantastic work ethic," he says. Boomers also have greater scheduling flexibility than college students—a selling point that is much appreciated by employers who are frequently left short-staffed by college students who must quit their jobs to return to school before the summer season officially ends.

Working in the national parks provides an experience that is more than just a job. "As gorgeous as it is in the parks, what makes them so special is the community spirit," says Bill. "People who work here tend to self-select. They share the same passions and values, and that makes for a strong community." In an environment where people eat, sleep, work, and socialize together, it's no surprise that strong bonds form. And it is not just couples that find it a welcome social scene. Singles, divorcees, and widows and widowers also enjoy the communal spirit, and Bill divulges that more than one late-life romance has flourished amid the forests and meadows.

Over the years, Bill has met many people whose lives were permanently changed by their time spent in the parks. Although their jobs lasted just a few short months, the experience left them with a lasting appreciation for nature, new places, and a different way of life. The fact that Bill gets to play a role in such a life-changing experience is one of the main reasons he derives such great joy from his work. He loves it when people meet him and say, "CoolWorks? CoolWorks changed my life!" Bill says that he keeps a fairy wand on his desk as a reminder that he gets to sprinkle magic into people's lives. "If someone comes out and is touched by nature, even if it is just for one summer, I like to think that the way they look at our planet will change," said Bill. "And that," he adds, "is crazy cool."

{continued}

Bill's Top Three Tips on Seasonal Employment

1. **Acquaint yourself with the full range of employment possibilities.** The parks aren't the only seasonal employers looking to staff their positions. CoolWorks.com posts job openings at fly-fishing lodges, dude ranches, adventure tour companies, the Nature Conservancy, and even the research stations in Antarctica.

2. **Don't assume all seasonal jobs are lower-level positions.** Most seasonal openings tend to be for positions like cooks, housekeeping staff, skilled-trades people, and maintenance workers. But employers also need people with professional backgrounds to work as hotel managers, food and beverage managers, bookkeepers, and accountants. Bill says that people with strong "management chops" may be able to find seasonal management jobs, especially if they have prior experience in the hospitality industry.

3. **Carefully research your housing options.** Many parks provide subsidized housing for their employees and try "within reason" to house older workers away from the "hormone-crazed twenty-something college students." Couples housing is available at many parks, but that tends to be limited, so many people opt to live in mobile homes, especially if they want to bring their pets along for the trip. You can find answers to your housing-related questions on the discussion forums and social networks hosted on CoolWorks.com.

In addition to the major job search boards and CoolWorks.com, here are some other useful seasonal-employment resources:

- American Camp Association (www.acacamps.org/jobs) maintains listings of both full-time and seasonal positions with summer camps.

- National Parks Association (www.nps.gov/personnel/index.htm)—the National Park Service hires up to ten thousand temporary and seasonal employees each year.

- SnagaJob.com and Seasonalemployment.com both specialize in seasonal job listings.

FIND A FREELANCE GIG

Earlier in this chapter, I emphasized that it is not always easy to find quality part-time and seasonal jobs. That is why many people chose to bypass the employee route in favor of work as independent contractors. The percentage of freelance workers is steadily growing as companies continue to outsource their noncore functions, and it is likely that many of you will work in a freelance capacity at some point in the future. A 2006 US government report issued by the Government Accountability Office (GAO) said that 31 percent of the workforce was independent or contingent workers, and by some estimates nearly half of the US job market will consist of freelance and temporary workers by 2020.

So who is using freelance workers? According to a 2011 survey conducted by the International Freelancers Academy, the majority of freelancers make their living providing business-to-business services with the remainder servicing individual consumers, nonprofits, government work, and associations. Your earning potential as an independent will vary tremendously depending upon your location, expertise, field, and specialty. The survey indicates that 45 percent of respondents earn between $20 and $59 per hour, and 26 percent earn anywhere from $80 to $200-plus per hour.

Many freelancers focus on a niche area as a way to distinguish their services from their competitors. For example, instead of offering generic writing services, you could specialize in writing website copy for recruiters. Or instead of working as a portrait photographer, you might specialize as a photographer who takes photos of homes for realtors or interior designers. When determining your niche, consider the following questions:

- Who would you most enjoy having as clients?

- What types of services or projects could you reasonably and effectively provide on a flexible basis?

- What is a niche that is not being adequately addressed by your competitors?

- Do you want to work for corporate clients or do you prefer small businesses?

- Are you willing to travel?

Life as a free agent can be a bit like a ride on a roller coaster, as you roll from high point to low point and back up again. On the upside, you can arrange your own schedule and be selective about the clients and projects that you choose. That level of freedom can be quite attractive to people who want to continue to use their professional or technical skills but don't want the restrictions associated with regular employment. On the downside, it can be challenging to find steady work, so you'll need to budget for the peaks and valleys associated with the freelance life. The constant need for marketing your services can get tiring (and frustrating), so if you're concerned about generating a sufficient stream of business on your own, you might consider teaming up with other freelancers to share projects and marketing responsibilities. As an independent contractor, you'll be responsible for paying your own taxes, tracking your business-related expenses, and handling all the administrative and marketing tasks needed to keep your business healthy—a juggling act that can sometimes prove challenging for people accustomed to the predictability of life as an employee of a larger organization.

But challenges aside, working on a freelance basis can also give you the freedom to try fun and unusual jobs that you might not have previously considered. In the following profile, you'll meet a woman who has created a whole new life for herself in her sixties, while juggling two very creative and enjoyable roles.

Profile of a Creative Free Agent

"I used to tell myself that I could never act or be in front of a camera. But I finally realized I was the only person saying 'I couldn't.' Why would I want to limit myself now?"
—Eve Young, celebrant and acting extra

For most of her adult life, Eve Young devoted herself to raising her children and being an active community volunteer, while also working as a part-time bookkeeper. But when her children grew up and left their home in Glen Ridge, New Jersey, Eve decided it was time for something new. For a while, she entertained thoughts of using her volunteer experience as a launching pad for a career in public service, but after serious consideration, she chose to explore other avenues instead.

One day, while reading her local paper, she learned about the Celebrant USA Foundation and Institute, a nonprofit organization that trains people to conduct ceremonies and officiate at life-cycle events. Eve was instantly drawn to the idea. As a woman who is part Native American, she had grown up around rituals and ceremonies, and the thought of helping other people commemorate milestone moments spoke to her in a very powerful way. She not only liked the idea but was confident that with her well-developed public speaking, interpersonal, and writing skills she could do the job well. "It all dovetailed so perfectly with my background," says Eve. She enrolled in the institute, and within a year's time had completed her training and was ordained as an interfaith minister.

Eve's clients come from all faiths and backgrounds and although some hire her simply to officiate and "make things legal," most want her to create one-of-a-kind ceremonies that reflect their unique heritage, vision, and value systems. As an example, Eve designed a wedding ceremony for a bride who was a single mom of Polish heritage and a groom who was African-American. The service included a traditional Polish blessing offered by the bride's grandmother, the groom's gifting the bride's daughter a charm bracelet as a token of his promise to care for her, and the reading of traditional African prayers. "I try to find readings for couples that are very personal so they are saying things that really mean something to them," says Eve, emphasizing that she never allows her own beliefs or values to influence the process. "The ceremony is all about them."

Eve's fee starts at $350 for a basic ceremony and goes up from there for more customized services. The initial meeting with clients typically lasts ninety minutes, but the actual writing of the ceremonies can require significantly more time. She officiates at an average of two events per month, a schedule that gives her plenty of time to write the ceremonies without feeling rushed—and allows her flexibility to pursue her other weekday job, working as a background actor.

Just as discovering the Celebrant USA Foundation was a serendipitous find, Eve's entry into acting was also a bit of a fluke. "I really wasn't interested in acting at all," she says, "but I needed to find a way to make some extra money to supplement the celebrant work." Once again, she discovered an opportunity through the newspaper—this time as the result of a classified advertising for acting extras. Despite having no prior acting experience, Eve went in for the interview and was hired as an extra on the set of the television show *Ugly Betty*. One assignment led to the next, and over time she has built up a steady flow of freelance work, finding opportunities through her agents and by responding to casting calls advertised online. Eve typically works anywhere from one to three days a week, although she says she could work more if she wanted to. She gets paid $75 to $125 per day for jobs on movie sets and at least $250 per day for jobs working as a model for print publications. If her jobs are secured through an agency, she pays the agency 10 to 15 percent of her fee. "I'm not getting rich and famous," she says, "but I'm meeting really interesting people and going places I wouldn't have otherwise."

Eve hopes one day to land a small recurring role on a television show. But whether or not she realizes that goal is secondary to the delight she feels at having found such a fun way to earn an income. "I'm working with really fascinating people," she says. "Doing this allows me to meet interesting people who don't always travel life in a straight line." Working in the creative world has given her other benefits as well, as she has learned to relax more, loosen up, and let go of her concerns about "what's dignified and the image I'm expected to portray." When I asked

Eve, who is sixty, how long she intended to continue working, she said she sees no end in sight, noting that she had recently worked on set with a woman who was seventy-five years old. "When I'm too old to stand up, I'll stop," laughs Eve, "but until then I plan to keep right on going."

Eve's Top Three Tips for Aspiring Acting Extras

1. **Be patient, but persistent.** It takes time to build up relationships with casting agencies and directors. Rejection is a big part of the acting profession—Eve says that she typically gets only one callback for every ten applications she submits.

2. **Use your age to your advantage.** Eve gets hired to play characters in the over-fifty age group. In an industry that is dominated by young starlets, her age gives her a marketing advantage. She has been advised by casting directors that she should leave her distinctive salt and pepper hair untouched; when they need an older person, they know to call Eve.

3. **Look for jobs online.** Eve finds jobs through sites like www .actorsaccess.com, www.nycastings.com, and www.castingnetworks .com, but she warns that you do need to be careful to choose your sites carefully. Although it is easiest to pursue this option if you live in New York or Los Angeles, other cities—such as Philadelphia, Miami, and Chicago, among others—have opportunities as well.

To learn more about the celebrant profession, visit the website of the Celebrant Institute and Foundation at www.celebrantinstitute.org. You can also read more about Eve's services at www.yourcelebrantceremony.com.

WORK-FROM-HOME GIGS

How nice would it be to collect a paycheck without having to leave the comfort of your own home? In our service-based global economy, almost any job that can be handled using a telephone and a computer can potentially be outsourced to a home-based worker. There was a time when "outsourcing" meant shipping jobs overseas, but these days many companies are shying away from the cultural and management challenges of offshoring, in favor of "homeshoring" jobs to home-based workers in the States. That's good news if you want to enjoy a paycheck that comes with the flexibility and portability of a work-from-home (or work-while-you-travel) arrangement.

At one time the domain of customer service representatives and telemarketers, the world of work-from-home jobs has expanded to include many professional level opportunities, including nurses who work for insurance companies, software designers, tax preparers, and others. Here is a small sampling of the types of virtual jobs you'll find advertised on the Internet:

- **Customer service and sales:** customer service agent, concierge services, sales representative, employment recruiter

- **Counseling and coaching services:** relocation counselor, camp or college adviser, job-search coach, employee assistance counselor, health coach

- **Computer-based work:** researcher, web designer, programmer, online tech support, translator, graphic designer, data entry operator, medical transcription/coding, legal researcher, online instructor, bookkeeper

- **Writing and editorial services:** copywriter, proofreader, editor, virtual assistant, online content provider, freelance writer

A small number of these jobs will provide you with company-sponsored benefits and/or office equipment, but those opportunities are limited. Be aware that the majority of the virtual jobs advertised are for people willing to work as independent contractors, not for people interested in full employment situations.

How to Find Virtual Jobs

- **Network.** Just like when you look for a "real" job, the best way to find work-at-home jobs is through your contacts. Make it a point to reach out to people you know who run their own businesses. Home-based entrepreneurs often lack the office space to house staff, so they are eager to outsource tasks like bookkeeping, telemarketing, and web design to home-based professionals. In general, assignments you find on your own through networking pay more than jobs advertised to the public.

- **Contact companies directly.** Most companies post their current job openings on their websites. But often the best opportunities go unadvertised, and as a result, it pays to approach companies directly as a way to find those hidden jobs before the competition arrives. You can do this one of two ways: either by networking your way into a personal introduction with a decision maker at the target company or by sending an e-mail and resume directly to the appropriate hiring department.

- **Find opportunities online.** Michael Haaren, cofounder of Ratracerebellion.com—an excellent source of virtual job listings, and publishers of a very useful free e-newsletter—recommends job aggregator sites such as Indeed.com and Simplyhired.com as legitimate sources of home-based jobs of all kinds. Haaren cautions that scams abound, so beware of promises of high income for little work, "no experience necessary," and "testiphonyals" (bogus testimonials), which often feature pirated photos. Again, remember the old adage, "If it sounds too good to be true, it probably is," and be very skeptical about paying money to sites promising online job listings.*

Sites that specialize in telecommuting and virtual jobs:

- Rat Race Rebellion (www.ratracerebellion.com)

- Telework Recruiting (www.teleworkrecruiting.com)

- FlexJobs (www.flexjobs.com)

---

*Both Telework Recruiting and FlexJobs charge a small fee for access to their sites, but in their case, I believe it is money well spent.

TEMPORARY AGENCIES

Many of you are probably familiar with the concept of working as a "temp," either because you worked as a temp at some point in your career or because you've hired a temp to help out in your own office. Temps have been used for years to fill administrative, clerical, and manual labor assignments, but companies now use temporary workers to fill professional jobs as well. Either way, it is a big business. According to statistics released in March 2012 by the American Staffing Association, in 2011 US staffing companies employed an average of nearly three million people per day.

Applying for work with a temporary agency is relatively easy. At many of the larger agencies, such as Manpower and Office Team, you can register and search for jobs online. If you opt to apply at an agency in person, you will probably be asked to fill out an application, take a skills test, and complete a brief intake interview. Your information will then be entered into a database and the agency will contact you when they have suitable openings. Some agencies provide benefits and many offer computer skills training.

To learn more: consult the classifieds section of your newspaper, search the online job boards, and take a look at the American Staffing Association (www.americanstaffing.net), which has a searchable database of agencies and an excellent collection of articles for temporary workers. Another useful site for finding temporary work opportunities is Net-Temps (www.net-temps.com).

INTERIM EXECUTIVE FIRMS

If you are a professional who still craves the challenges of executive life, you'll be interested to know that during the past decade a new and more elite model of talent-on-demand services, known as "interim executive firms," has gained hold in the United States. Interim executive firms contract with senior-level executives to assist companies in need of "leadership on demand." Interim executives handle a variety of assignments: filling in for an executive on leave, managing projects that can't be handled by in-house staff, or helping less experienced leaders with navigating through a transition or merger. Companies use interim executive firms for part-time assistance when they can't afford to hire an executive on a full-time basis; private equity firms also use interim executives to help manage and restructure their start-up ventures.

If your resume includes experience as a senior-level executive, consultant, or business owner, you may be well positioned to work with an interim executive services firm. Life as an interim executive gives you the opportunity to work on interesting assignments, earn a professional salary, and participate in high-level projects while enjoying time off in between assignments. It is an intriguing option for people who still want to enjoy the adrenaline, excitement, and challenges of the executive life after leaving their full-time jobs.

To help you gain a better understanding of what interim executive services firms look for in their employees and contractors, I turned to Karen MacLeod, a pioneer in the executive services industry who is currently president of Tatum LLC, a US-based executive services firm.

ADVICE FROM THE INTERIM EXECUTIVE EXPERT

"This is a growing trend; companies are much more comfortable now hiring high-level variable workers. You can make a good permanent living being a variable worker."

—KAREN MACLEOD, president, Tatum LLC

What type of employees does your firm hire?
K.M: We seek executives with broad-based accounting and finance experience. We like interesting personalities who can learn, adapt

{continued}

quickly to a number of different types of client environments, and easily build relationships with new clients.

Are your interim executives considered employees or independent contractors?

K.M: They are considered employees who work for Tatum on a project-to-project basis. Compensation is competitive with the market standard for full-time employment. Health insurance is offered after a sixty-day waiting period.

Why are executive services firms a good fit for people over fifty who want flexibility?

K.M: We only hire seasoned talent, and as a result, almost all of our employees are at least forty years old. In truth, because our business flow is subject to fluctuations, we prefer employees who aren't looking for a full-time schedule year round; it is more stressful for us to work with people who have a mortgage to pay and need a guarantee of a full-time salary. Interestingly many of our older workers tell us that now that they are empty nesters, they actually enjoy the opportunity to travel to different parts of the country. It can be a nice way to get to live in different cities without having to pay for travel out of your own pocket.

Do all assignments require travel?

K.M: There is a lot of travel with this type of work, but you don't have to travel all the time. Increasingly we have opportunities for employees to work from home, at least part of the time.

What advice do you have for people who want to work as interim executives?

K.M: We look for talented and experienced people who embrace change and strive to remain relevant, valuable, vibrant, and creative. If you are that type of person, we will work hard to keep you on assignments.

How much flexibility can you realistically offer employees?

K.M: When our employees are on assignment, we expect them to work the same hours they would as if they were permanent staff. We are fond of saying, "Don't look at it as if you are an interim; look at it as you are the CFO." But in between assignments, the employee is free to pursue other interests. It's a great fit for people who want to take blocks of time off between projects. Obviously the more parameters someone places around when they can work, the more challenging it can be to place them on assignment, but we try hard to accommodate the needs of our top talent. Our people are our business; retaining our best people is a key priority for us.

Karen's Top Three Tips for Working as an Interim Executive

1. **Spend time tweaking your resume to showcase your full range of experience.** Your skills are important, but we are even more interested in your ability to adapt to a number of different types of situations, personalities, and work environments.

2. **Invest in your professional presence.** It's important to look and act current. Be willing to update your wardrobe and invest in learning new technologies—texting is no longer just for your kids or grandkids!

3. **Realize that attitude trumps ability.** A good attitude is the single most important thing. We look for people who are flexible, open-minded, and happy to work with a diverse group of people.

To find interim executive services firms in your area of expertise, start with a Google search and by asking colleagues for recommendations of reputable firms. Most firms advertise their services on the major job boards.

THREE KEY CONSIDERATIONS ON TRADING YOUR TIME FOR A PAYCHECK

1. **Benefits.** Part-time jobs can sometimes provide a useful way to secure benefits after leaving a full-time employer. Although the number of companies that offer part-time benefits is limited, and in most cases you will need to work at least thirty hours per week to qualify for them, part-time benefit packages can include health insurance, paid holidays, vacations, 401(k) plans, and company discounts. Large retailers like Costco, chains like Starbucks, and many hospitals offer good part-time benefit packages. Be sure to check the websites of companies you like for more information.

2. **Hours.** Working part-time can be wonderful, but be careful to avoid situations in which employers try to squeeze full-time responsibilities into part-time hours. Ask questions that give you a good understanding about your expected job duties and responsibilities before you accept any position.

3. **Lifestyle objectives.** There are always tradeoffs involved in every work situation. A part-time job provides the security of a paycheck but doesn't provide the freedom associated with being on your own; a temp job gives you needed income, but you have to continually adjust to new work environments; and seasonal employment provides variety but also includes periods of time when you will earn no income. Be clear in your own mind about what is most important to you—and your lifestyle objectives—before you go looking for part-time income solutions.

CHAPTER SIX

Make a Living While Making a Difference

For many people approaching retirement, earning income may now be a secondary goal compared to the desire to make a difference in the world. They don't want to just leave a legacy; they want to live one! If that is true for you, consider yourself in very good company. According to a 2011 study by Civic Ventures, a nonprofit think tank on boomers, work, and social purpose, as many as nine million people aged forty-four to seventy are already working in "encore careers" that combine personal meaning, social impact, and continued income; and an additional thirty-one million people in the same age group say they are interested in finding encore career–related work. That means roughly 40 percent of all boomers hope to be able to find a way to give back through their second-act careers. As a career coach who specializes in working with older adults, I find these statistics to be in line with my own client experience. Indeed, the majority of my second-act clients express a strong desire to find work that will enable them to leave a more meaningful mark on the world.

In this chapter, we will examine different ways you can use your second act to create your own encore career. But before we get into the specifics, I want to emphasize that doing "good" work doesn't mean you are restricted to working for a nonprofit or in the public sector. Not everyone can, or should, go to work for a nonprofit, and if you consider only nonprofit paths, you may end up shortchanging both yourself and the greater world around you. As I am fond of saying to my clients: "You don't need to be Mother Teresa to a make a difference in the world. Mother Teresa needed to be Mother Teresa. You need to make a difference by honoring *your* unique gifts."

Thankfully no single industry, organization, or profession offers the one right path to making a difference in our world; every endeavor holds the potential to make the world a better place. A fashion designer makes a difference when she donates her dresses to students who otherwise wouldn't be able to attend the prom. An architect who designs a cancer center that fosters emotional, spiritual, and physical healing makes a difference to people dealing with life-threatening illness. And a successful entrepreneur who creates new jobs makes a difference by giving people a way to support themselves and their families.

Each of these professionals makes a significant contribution to the world through her or his respective talents—and you can too. At a time when there are so many problems to be solved in our world, our nation, and in our local communities, there has never been a better moment to put your experiences and wisdom to good use.

WORK FOR A NONPROFIT ORGANIZATION

Having just insisted that you don't need to work for a nonprofit organization in order to make a difference, I present this option first because it is the one most people think of when they consider doing good works. The nonprofit world is vast and diverse; it includes charities, advocacy groups, foundations, religious institutions, arts groups, universities, hospitals, associations, and unions. According to Independent Sector, a leadership network for the nonprofit and philanthropic communities, nonprofits and foundations play a major role in our economy; they employ 9 percent of the American workforce and account for 5 percent of our gross domestic product.

Whether you want to work for a museum, a charity, or an advocacy group, it is likely you will find the experience of working at a nonprofit somewhat different from your experience in the for-profit sector. On the positive side, nonprofits are generally regarded as nice places to work: kindness, passion, and purpose are more highly valued than in profit-driven companies, work schedules tend be more flexible, and the joy of working for a mission-driven organization is a welcome change for people accustomed to putting profits before people. That said, working at a nonprofit is not always an ideal situation. Most organizations still have their share of office politics (people are people, after all), and the realities of working with a limited budget, a volunteer staff, and a dependency on erratic funding sources can prove problematic and stressful.

Consequently, if you think you want to work for a nonprofit, take the time to consider your options before applying for work. Carefully assess your skills, experience, and interests, and then begin to explore ways you can best use your skills in organizations that appeal to you. It can be helpful to first volunteer or serve on a nonprofit board as a way to become familiar with an organization and its culture before committing to a more permanent employment relationship.

To help you gain a better understanding of what your transition into the nonprofit world might involve, I interviewed Barbara Salop, age fifty-eight, a career IBM executive who recently made her own transition into the nonprofit world.

From IBM Executive to Nonprofit Consultant

"People think there aren't many good business people in the non-profit world, but there are wonderful people—they just have a whole lot less to work with than people in the corporate world."
—Barbara Salop, nonprofit consultant

Barbara Salop, a former client of mine from Riverside, Connecticut, has long been a strong supporter of organizations that benefit people with developmental disabilities. But because she was a full-time working mother of two, the number of hours Barbara was able to devote to volunteer activities was restricted by the demands of work and family. So in 2010, when she was able to retire with full benefits from IBM, Barbara decided to take her executive expertise and apply it to the nonprofit sector. Recognizing that she needed to get some serious nonprofit experience in order to strengthen her credentials and her familiarity with the nonprofit world, Barbara spent eighteen months working as a pro bono consultant for several local nonprofits. She then applied for and was accepted into the Hartford Encore Fellows program, a workforce development program that helps seasoned professionals transition into the nonprofit sector. That program gave her an opportunity to immerse herself in the nonprofit world through classroom training, job shadowing, and a two-month internship experience. It also gave her a chance to get to know people actively working in the sector, as well as build a peer group of other executives who were also actively transitioning into the nonprofit sector. At the time I interviewed Barbara, she was starting her first paid consulting assignment with an organization she had originally worked for as a volunteer. I asked Barbara for her impressions of the nonprofit arena:

What are the most striking differences between life at IBM and the nonprofit world?

B.S: There are lots of similarities, but also plenty of differences. In corporate, it is all about making money, but in nonprofits, the focus is on the mission. Nonprofits sometimes make decisions that seem nonbusiness-like to the rest of us, but they represent tradeoffs that reflect their determination to put the mission before the money. It takes great discipline to make those tough choices, especially when funding is scarce. I have the deepest admiration for that level of commitment to a cause.

Did you notice a difference in the types of people who work for profit versus nonprofit?

B.S: I was very impressed by how happy most of the nonprofit executives seem to be. I don't mean to make it sound like it is always perfect in a Pollyanna-like way, but there was a real sense of mission, purpose, and fulfillment among the people I met. Even when they were having a tough day, it was clear that they have an underlying sense of happiness about what they are doing. Although I had many good days at IBM, and was proud of what my team accomplished, I rarely experienced that same sense of deep fulfillment from my corporate work.

How did the nonprofits where you volunteered react to you being a "corporate" person?

B.S: That was interesting. On one hand, there seemed to be some trepidation about a corporate person walking into a nonprofit. Their perception is that corporate types are only about the numbers, and we make decisions based on measurements and profits alone. On the other hand, some people are almost awestruck by people from corporate and [practically] treat us like we are from a different planet. I found it to be so important to take the time to listen to what they had to say, learn from them, and respect their expertise.

There are so many ways to volunteer. How did you decide which organizations to approach about volunteering?

B.S: I knew that I wanted to focus on working with organizations that support people with developmental disabilities, so I targeted those types of opportunities. In terms of what you choose to do for them, there are essentially two ways to help. One is to do the easy, hands-on things like stuffing envelopes or serving at a soup kitchen. It is needed work, and they will appreciate your time. But if you are an experienced businessperson, I think you owe it to the nonprofit to find a way to leverage your professional expertise. They are so grateful when you can help them do the things they can't do or don't have the time to do, like project management, facilitation, or strategic planning.

After being a long-term volunteer, how did you broach the subject of getting paid for your work?

B.S: I hung around long enough for them to really value my business expertise! When you can get them to see your value proposition and understand the business case for your fees, it is a much easier sell. Even once I was done with projects, I checked in with my volunteer sites to follow up with them about their implementation plans. Over time they realized that it would pay to keep me around. I think it also is helpful to offer your services as an independent contractor instead of expecting the organization to hire you. In this economy, if they have the option of bringing in a variable worker, it makes sense for them to do that. It may cost them a bit more in the short term, but it gives them greater long-term flexibility.

How did you know what to charge?

B.S: Quite honestly, it was difficult to know what to charge. I asked my friends in nonprofits who had previously hired consultants for their suggestions. I was willing to start with a low rate because I knew I still had a lot to learn and I needed to get some more experience in the sector. I suspect that as I continue to contribute and add value, there will be opportunities for me to raise my rates.

What suggestions do you have regarding the nonprofit job search?

B.S: Like any job search, networking is critically important, and I spent a lot of time on that. Sometimes I felt like I was just going for endless cups of coffee, but it paid off in the end. In terms of resources, LinkedIn is an invaluable tool that I used to identify board members and volunteers at organizations that appealed to me.

Do you have any additional thoughts for people considering making a switch to nonprofits?

B.S: Take your time in determining the types of organizations you want to work for. You are going to get paid a lot less than you earned in corporate, so find a sector that really speaks to you. This transition can take longer than you anticipate, but have faith that it will be worth the effort.

Here are five excellent resources to help you make the transition into the nonprofit sector:

1. **Encore.org (www.encore.org).** If you are over forty and want to get involved in helping to make the world a better place, you owe it to yourself to get familiar with both Civic Ventures and Encore.org. Civic Ventures funds a number of initiatives, fellowships, and programs designed to help boomers solve serious social problems (including the fellowship program Barbara attended). The Encore.org website, published by Civic Ventures, is the single most comprehensive resource for boomers interested in careers that combine personal meaning, social impact, and continued income. Their outstanding guide to encore careers can be downloaded for free at www.encore.org/files/PDFs/guide/encore_guide.pdf. Marc Freedman, the CEO and founder of Civic Ventures, wrote the book *Encore: Finding Work That Matters in the Second Half of Life* (PublicAffairs, 2008)—it is a compelling read for anyone interested in this subject.

2. **Bridgestar (www.bridgestar.org).** Bridgestar.org is a site for seasoned executives who want to transition from the for-profit sector into nonprofits. They have an extensive career center and a job board that lists both staff jobs and nonprofit board positions.

3. **Idealist (www.idealist.org).** Idealist.org is a must-visit for anyone interested in exploring the world of nonprofits. The site features career advice, a job board, and information about events, fellowships, internships, volunteer opportunities, and educational programs in the nonprofit world.

4. **The Foundation Center (www.foundationcenter.org).** Whether you want to establish a foundation, learn how to write a grant, or secure funds for research, this is the right site for you. The Foundation Center is the leading source of information about philanthropy worldwide, with a site that lists training programs, job openings, and other useful resources.

5. **National Council of Nonprofit Associations (www.councilof nonprofits.org).** The National Council of Nonprofit Associations is the network of state and regional nonprofit associations serving more than twenty thousand member organizations. Although this site is geared toward nonprofit administrators, their resources will help educate you about key issues relevant to smaller nonprofit organizations.

Finally, if you want to stay up-to-date on the latest news in the world of philanthropy, a great resource is the *Chronicle of Philanthropy* (philanthropy.com). It is both in print and online, and it is like the *New York Times* of the philanthropy world.

SERVE IN THE PEACE CORPS

Have you ever thought about serving in the Peace Corps but assumed you'd missed your chance when you didn't enroll right after college? Well, think again! Now might be the perfect time to recapture that long-lost dream. Contrary to what most people think, the Peace Corps is not just for recent college graduates. More than 5 percent of Peace Corps volunteers are over age fifty, and at the time this book was written, the oldest serving Peace Corps volunteer was eighty years old! (You may remember reading about the Peace Corps's most famous older volunteer, Miss Lillian, President Jimmy Carter's mother, who served in India at age sixty-eight.)

The use of the word "volunteer" is a bit misleading, because the Peace Corps does pay volunteers a monthly stipend and a readjustment allowance. They also provide comprehensive health insurance and round-trip transportation to and from the destination country. After you complete your service, if you later apply for federal jobs you will receive preferential treatment; there are also opportunities for graduate school scholarships, fellowships, and internships.

Life in the Peace Corps isn't known for being easy, but it can be a highly rewarding, deeply meaningful, and life-changing experience.

Volunteers are needed with expertise in a number of different areas, including education, youth and community development, information technology, agriculture, environment, business development, and health-related issues. Following a careful vetting process, the Peace Corps will determine where you will serve and what you will be asked to do; you will be placed with the host country that can best use your skills. Volunteers commit to a twenty-seven-month service term, which includes a three-month immersion-training program to learn a new language, technical skills, and cultural considerations. Upon completing your training, you'll live in the community you serve, which could be a small village, a medium-size town, or a bustling urban environment.

People who are interested in pursuing this option need to plan ahead. The application process can take nine months to a year, and not all applicants are accepted (note that 90 percent of applicants have a college degree). All applicants undergo a thorough and rigorous medical and dental assessment to determine whether they are medically qualified to serve—an evaluation that, if you have preexisting conditions or a complicated medical history, can take longer and require additional medical testing. The Peace Corps does accept married couples, but the placement process will likely take longer, and there must be a suitable assignment for each applicant in the same location.

To learn more, visit the special section on the Peace Corps website specifically for applicants over fifty: www.peacecorps.gov/50plus. Another helpful resource is *The Insider's Guide to the Peace Corps* by Dillon Banerjee (Ten Speed Press, 2009).

CREATE YOUR OWN NONPROFIT

Have you been frustrated in your efforts to locate the perfect nonprofit employer? It can be harder than you expect to find the right match. That is why for some people the best way to give back is to create their own nonprofit organization, foundation, or charity. Starting your own nonprofit can be a wonderful way to support initiatives that you really care about, especially when they are not being adequately addressed by existing foundations or charities. But as with any start-up venture, the effort involved with getting your new nonprofit organization up and running is considerable, and with over one and a half million nonprofits already vying for funding, attention, and volunteers, you'll want to ensure that the one you start is unique enough to thrive in a competitive marketplace. It can take several years before you're able to fund salaries, especially your own, so this is an option that works best when you have an alternate source of income to sustain you during the start-up phase. It can be a challenge to run these organizations, so plan on working long hours, at least until you are able to get the organization on a solid footing.

To help you gain a better understanding of what it might be like to run your own nonprofit, I interviewed two women who created their own nonprofit endeavors. They represent two very different types of organizations, but in each case, the woman is having a wonderful time working hard on a cause she cares passionately about. Their energy, dedication, and creativity are truly remarkable.

From Artist to Activist: A "Hag" on a Mission

"It's amazing to live a life that is aligned with one's purpose. My purpose is to make art and promote artists who would otherwise not be seen. It's been a fast and fun ride, with each day getting better and better."

—Terri Lloyd, cofounder of the Haggus Society,
  Highland Park, California

Since she was a little girl, Terri Lloyd loved creating art. But as is true for so many women of her generation, the need to balance her roles as a mom, wife, and full-time worker (in Terri's case, as a marketing professional) left her little free time to devote to her fine art. As she approached her fiftieth birthday, Terri felt a strong desire to pursue her art on a more full-time basis. With her husband's blessing and support, she made the decision to leave the traditional nine-to-five workplace behind.

While transitioning into life as a working artist, Terri began to wonder whether there was funding available to help support older women artists like herself. But the more she explored, the more discouraged she became. Instead of discovering exciting scholarships and grants, her research revealed that there was surprisingly little institutional support for women who had put their artistic pursuits on hold for families and career. Terri knew she was not the only reemerging artist struggling with the lack of funding. Indeed, most of her women artist friends had taken time away from their creative pursuits to raise families. Once she realized the full scope of the funding problem, Terri was angered—and motivated—enough to put aside her desire to immerse herself in her own art and instead refocused her energies on creating a better support net for her fellow female artists.

Working together with her best friend, artist Monica Marsh, Terri formed the Haggus Society, a membership-based organization for older women artists "with an edge," whose creative endeavors don't necessarily fit into the "hygienic mold of what is perceived to be feminine." The name Haggus is a play on words that resulted from a conversation between the two founders when one of them noted, "We need something for 'old hags like us'!" Thanks to her prior experience working for a nonprofit arts group, Terri was able to get the society organized and off the ground quickly. She knew how to approach sponsors and apply for grants, and as a skilled marketer she also was able to quickly attract publicity and media attention.

By the end of their first year of operation, the group had secured a fiscal sponsor, enrolled their first forty members, and launched several exhibitions. Membership dues in the Haggus Society range from $50 for low and limited income members up to $500 for lifetime membership. Benefits of membership include opportunities to participate in juried shows, peer reviews, marketing services, and educational programs. Initially envisioned as strictly for midlife and older women, the makeup of the organization has evolved over time. "We have attracted attention from some younger women and some men as well," says Terri.

"It's interesting to see where it goes. I am open to whoever wants to jump on board."

Terri is not currently earning an income from her nonprofit, but she anticipates drawing a salary within three years. According to Terri, it takes about three years to build up enough of a track record to qualify for the big funding sources. In the meantime, she helps support herself through the sale of her art (and her husband's financial backing). When the organization does apply for the more significant grants, they will be required to have a paid executive director on staff, and Terri anticipates that she will fill that role.

As exciting as this new venture is, Terri is already thinking about her exit plan, determined not to overstay her welcome and hoping to eventually have more time to devote to her own art. "I want the organization to stay fresh and current," says Terri, noting that five years from now she wants to cede her leadership role to someone who can keep the organization robust and vibrant. But until that happens, she is energized and enthusiastic about continuing to work to develop the organization. "I am having the time of my life. I really am," she says. "It's amazing to be doing this thing that is all about my passion for the arts and my desire to give women, particularly women over forty, a voice in the arts."

Terri's Top Three Tips for Creating a Nonprofit

1. **Develop a plan and a strategy.** You need a plan, even if it is a loose one. Terri has what she calls "a living document" posted on her wall: a month-to-month guide to her goals and action plan. She continuously evaluates what is working and what is not, and she adjusts as she goes along.

2. **Do your homework.** Learn what it takes to put together a nonprofit, and educate yourself about what it takes to write a grant.

3. **Be patient.** Terri says, "Success isn't one big shebang; it is many small steps, lots of failures, and the accumulation of the learning along the way. All roads lead to someplace. Everything I've learned in my life has contributed to this moment."

A Recipe for Nonprofit Success

"If you had told me in 2005, when I rolled into my first classroom to give a cooking class, that only six years later I would be designing an e-learning website, have dozens of employees, and be taking our program to a national scale, I would never have dreamed it."
—Gracie Cavnar, founder and president, Recipe for Success

Obesity is a serious and growing epidemic that threatens our nation's future. The latest statistics indicate that more than 30 percent of American children are overweight and at risk of developing obesity. In Texas, where Gracie Cavnar lives, nearly 50 percent of fourth graders fall into an at-risk weight category. But while most of us simply worry about the impact of this epidemic, Gracie decided that talk alone wasn't going to solve anything. A vibrant woman, with significant professional and volunteer experience, she knew that she had the resources, connections, and personal determination needed to make a difference—she just needed to figure out the best way to make it happen.

Gracie set out to learn everything she could about the obesity problem, a research project that took nearly ten years to complete. Initially she planned to use funds from her family foundation to help finance other people's foundations and initiatives. But the more she learned, the more determined she became to play a bigger role in the solution. That determination, along with funding from Gracie's family foundation, led to the establishment of the Recipe for Success (RFS) Foundation, a 501(c)(3) organization dedicated to combating childhood obesity by changing the way our children understand, appreciate, and eat their food.

Using a curriculum designed to make learning about good food fun, RFS focuses on preventing obesity by teaching children healthy eating habits before obesity sets in. The concept behind RFS is a simple one: when children become familiar with food from "seed to table"—planting the seeds, harvesting the crops, and cooking the food—it can change the way they eat for the rest of their lives. As children experience the difference between how processed food and real food tastes, they start paying more attention to what and how they are eating, and that results in healthier lifelong eating patterns. According to the RFS website, "children need to learn that food doesn't grow in drive-through windows and plastic wrapping; that a Twinkie is not a vegetable."

The RFS foundation launched with a pilot program in five Houston elementary schools. One of their first offerings was Chefs in Schools, a monthly cooking class taught with the assistance of twenty-four volunteer professional chefs from the Houston area. Using tools, ingredients, and lessons provided by RFS, the children worked together with the chefs to blend pesto, bake muffins, and cook ratatouille. (The food was harvested by the students from gardens that were built in each of the pilot schools.) For some of the students, it was the first time they had ever eaten meals prepared with entirely fresh food, and for all the students it proved to be a memorable culinary experience.

What started as a pilot program run by Gracie, her assistant, and a group of dedicated volunteers quickly extended to many more Houston area schools. In their second year, RFS also began to offer monthlong summer camps for third to fifth graders and special nutrition classes for parents of infants and toddlers. Today Gracie oversees a paid staff of over twenty-five employees, and, working in collaboration with the Presidential Task Force on Childhood Obesity, RFS is developing an e-learning website that will provide remote teacher training and certification of their Seed-to-Plate Nutrition Education programs in affiliate locations across the United States. Future plans on the drawing board include a national television program and a companion series of cookbooks.

Not surprisingly Gracie and her foundation have attracted attention and accolades from a distinguished group of admirers, including the mayor of Houston, Dr. Mehmet Oz, and even President Obama. In 2011, *Self* magazine honored Gracie as a recipient of their Women Doing Good award. Gracie is both flattered and humbled by the recognition, but she stressed that the press is most important because it brings attention to the work of the foundation and the problems of obesity. "I am always deeply thankful when somebody notices," she says. "If I can inspire someone else who has the time and ability to help, that is a big deal because there is so much that needs to be done." The success of RFS can be credited to many different factors, but the fact that Gracie was a seasoned volunteer who had previously volunteered for dozens of philanthropic endeavors in the Houston area has proved invaluable. As an experienced volunteer, she understood the best way to structure her own nonprofit and was very familiar with the demands of managing a volunteer organization.

Nonetheless, the road to success hasn't been without its challenges. Managing an organization with twenty-five employees (and counting) has been a self-described stretch for Gracie, who in her former careers as a model, architect, and journalist had always purposefully avoided being a manager. But as the director of an evolving organization, Gracie realized that if she wanted RFS to be more than just a "flash in the pan," she needed to learn to thrive outside her comfort zone. "It's been a real growth path for me," she notes, "learning in my mid-fifties how to manage an organization, how to create and execute a long-range plan, and how to scale our program for a national audience." As the foundation's full-time executive director, Gracie admits that she is running "full-tilt" (Gracie's husband retired nine months after she started RFS, but because she was so busy, he decided to return to work) and indicated that she thought she was about a year away from being able to cut back to a more part-time schedule. In spite of the long hours involved with running a nonprofit, Gracie has never felt more alive; she is impassioned by her mission and believes that others can experience that same wonderful sense of satisfaction from engaging in meaningful work. To learn more about Recipe for Success, visit www.recipe4success.org.

Gracie's Top Three Tips for Working in the Nonprofit World

1. **Value your business skills.** There is no shortage of people who have enthusiasm and dedication for meaningful causes, but it takes people with solid business skills to make a nonprofit successful. Broad-based business skills like accounting, HR, and marketing are always needed; administrative and office skills are also highly valued.

2. **Embrace a "roll up your sleeves" attitude.** There is a lot of fluff built into corporate. But in nonprofits, you've got to be a real renaissance person who can juggle many different tasks. "It is important to be nimble and organic in response to the market," says Gracie. "You have to have your head up at all times in order to adapt to what is going on."

3. **Don't plan an organization around the founder.** Like Terri Lloyd, Gracie also emphasizes that the organization needs to be able to thrive whether or not she is there. "That should be the goal of any organization," she says.

To learn more: Managing a nonprofit requires fund-raising, organizational, and management skills, along with an understanding of the administrative, legal, and tax side of the nonprofit world. Fortunately many colleges offer courses in nonprofit management that can help educate you on the basics for success. The Foundation Center at www.foundationcenter.org is another helpful resource. The US Small Business Administration has posted links of federal programs and services useful to nonprofits at www.sba.gov/content/nonprofit-organizations.

CREATE PROFITS WITH A PURPOSE

Even though not everyone is cut out to work for a nonprofit, that doesn't mean you can't still find a way to give back through for-profit pursuits. Many of the people interviewed for this book have found creative ways to make a positive difference in the world through their businesses: by mentoring others, using their work to give voice to an important message, donating a portion of their profits to charity, or creating a service that makes life easier, better, or safer. Their commitment to run their businesses with a focus on making the world a better place both inspired and impressed me. I think they will do the same for you.

Four Socially-Minded Entrepreneurs

Anita Mahaffey, CEO of Cool-jams, San Diego, California

How she makes a difference:

- Donates 20 percent of profits to charities

- Volunteers to mentor new entrepreneurs

Back when she was a high school student, Anita Mahaffey spent a year as a foreign exchange student in Turkey. At the time, it was simply a fun thing to do. But that trip ultimately played a major role in her career path, not just once but twice over the course of a thirty-year period. The first connection happened when Anita traveled back to Turkey after starting her family. While there, she visited with friends who took her on a tour of their factory, and as a result of that visit, she started a business importing bathrobes from Turkey. Anita's business ran successfully for a number of years, but as she approached her late forties, she decided to "retire" in order to spend more time with her family and volunteer activities.

During her "retirement," Anita took yet another trip back to Turkey, and once again, inspiration struck. While visiting with her former Turkish partners, she learned that they were manufacturing a new microfiber fabric that wicks moisture away from the body. As an avid hiker and runner, she was already familiar with the benefits of wearing microfiber apparel to stay warm and dry. But when Anita, who was suffering with hot flashes at that time, felt the fabric, she thought, "Why not use this to make pajamas that help keep menopausal women comfortable while they sleep?" Excited by the idea, Anita took a sample piece of the fabric home, and after bringing it to an independent laboratory that tested and confirmed the fabric's quick-drying capabilities, she was convinced that she had a winning business concept in hand.

Ever the entrepreneur, Anita decided to abandon retirement and reenter the business world. She launched Cool-jams (www.cool-jams .com) as an online store in 2008, and, despite a challenging economy, the business took off and has been profitable ever since. The site now sells bedding products and pajamas for a growing customer base of travelers, nursing mothers, and people suffering from night sweats caused by chemotherapy, obesity, menopause, and other medical issues. As the business grows, she is actively investigating ways to expand her distribution to other retail outlets.

One of the things Anita, now age fifty-three, appreciates most about her business is that it allows her to share her success with others less fortunate. Each year she donates 20 percent of the company's profits to charities focused on women and families. In just three years' time, the company has donated nearly $35,000 to charities. Anita hopes there will be many more donations in the years to come. "When we make money, we are able to give more," said Anita. "It is a win-win for everyone." In addition to donating a percentage of her business profits, Anita volunteers her time mentoring other entrepreneurs and sharing her business expertise. It is an activity that she undertakes with equal parts joy, gratitude, and obligation. "I think it is important to use our gifts to give something back," says Anita. "For me, I am good at starting businesses, so that is how I can make a contribution. I can give with my time, my products, and my profits. It makes me really happy to be able to do that."

Dewey Crepeau, J.D., director of A Gift of Hope Adoption Agency, Columbia, Missouri

How he makes a difference:

- Unites children in need with parents who want children

- Donates his expertise to nonprofit adoption organizations

As a young lawyer starting out in private practice in Columbia, Missouri, Dewey Crepeau worked on a variety of legal issues. Most of his caseload revolved around criminal and civil matters, but every once in a while he was given responsibility for managing an adoption case. Out of all his assignments, Dewey enjoyed the adoptions most. However, as much as he loved those types of cases, he couldn't afford to work on them full-time; he had a family to support and couldn't restrict his practice to just adoptions.

But after his children grew up and his daughter earned a master's degree in social work, Dewey finally got the chance he had been waiting for. In a case of "like father, like daughter," his daughter decided that she wanted to go to work for an adoption agency. At the time, she was unable to find work with an agency in St. Louis, but in her efforts to find a job, she connected with a woman from California, Tina Tyra, who was involved in adoption counseling on the West Coast. As luck would have it, Tina was interested in the possibility of establishing an adoption agency in the Midwest. The two of them started talking, and it wasn't long before they turned to Dewey for advice about opening an agency. Dewey was finally at a point in his own career when he was ready to focus on adoption cases. After many conversations (and lots of paperwork), the three of them teamed up to establish A Gift of Hope Adoptions agency in 2005.

Dewey now earns his living as the executive director of the agency while also maintaining a small private practice on the side. His daughter works as the director of placement services (primarily working from home while caring for three small children), and Tina, who still lives in California, functions as their West Coast adoption and communication consultant. Dewey, now age fifty-seven, is delighted that after all these years he is able to apply his professional expertise to an arena that means so much to him. (And as an added bonus, he also gets to spend more time with his daughter.) Although he could earn more doing other types of work, he knows that his legal expertise makes a very real difference to both the children and the parents involved in the adoptions, and no matter how many cases he handles, he never tires of the joy he feels each time after helping to place a child in need with a loving family.

Lisa Dudley, singer and performer, Troy, New York

How she makes a difference:

- Promotes inspiration, hope, and healing through her music

- Performs benefit concerts for veterans

Lisa Dudley was "born singing." Growing up, she sang at Girl Scout events, in the choir, and at church. She planned to major in music in college—a plan that was derailed after she transferred schools, got married, and started working, first as a secretary and later as a home mortgage loan officer. Even though music took a back seat to earning a living, she still always found a way to keep music in her life: singing, writing songs, and performing whenever and wherever she could.

When her father fell ill and needed surgery, she sang to him in the recovery room, moving the attending nurses to tears. "That was when it really hit me that my singing affects people in very profound ways," says Lisa. She traveled to Nashville, where she recorded her unique blend of country, gospel, and folk songs. Lisa's music is about hope: hope for war veterans struggling with their injuries, hope for patients recovering from illness, and hope for older women coming to terms with their changing bodies and circumstances. Lisa says her goal is to use her music to help move people from darkness into a place of joy.

Over the years, Lisa divorced, moved to upstate New York, and remarried. Now, at age fifty, she is finally able to focus more of her energies on building her music career. She sells her CDs at her performances and online through CDBaby.com. Lisa is also promoting her scores for use in television and movies, and she trusts that, with time, she will be able to earn a full-time income from her music. She is performing more frequently and has donated the proceeds from some of her concerts to organizations that work with veterans' groups. She is also hoping to find a major Latin artist to record the Spanish version of her song *I Believe in America*, a project that has been encouraged by her Latino friends who want to have an inspirational patriotic song recorded in their native tongue.

Susan Nisinzweig, founder, EytanArt.com, Riverside, Connecticut

How she makes a difference:

- Anti-bullying advocate

- Donates a percentage of profits to charities

Susan Nisinzweig's oldest son, Eytan, is a twenty-five year-old man with autism. Although he has limited social skills, Eytan is a gifted artist who draws with a simple and captivating style that reflects a childlike wonder of the world. For many years, Susan, a social worker by training, thought about doing something special with Eytan's art, but her good intentions never translated into action—that is, until one day when she began to consider the possibility of pairing Eytan's drawings with inspirational sayings. She began to wonder whether she could have phrases that celebrate our differences, encourage civility, and promote respect for others printed on products like T-shirts and posters, and the more she thought about this idea, the more excited she became.

Looking back on that moment, Susan knew she had found her mission. "The thrill, or shiver was unmistakable, and the ideas were so powerful that this time they didn't disappear down the drain of the shower," said Susan. "I knew that this was one of those ideas that I had to make a reality. I knew that this one really mattered and was what I was meant to do." With focus, drive, and determination, the pieces of the entrepreneurial puzzle quickly began to fall into place. Although Susan had no prior experience with the retail clothing business, she researched the worlds of shirt manufacturing, online sales, and internet marketing. Talking to anyone who would listen, and adjusting plans as she learned, Susan quickly found a printer to produce the shirts, built a website, and launched her business selling EytanArt's products online, at craft fairs, and at fund-raising events.

The reaction to Eytan's work has been overwhelmingly positive, and orders have come in from around the globe. In addition to championing a message that celebrates differences, Susan delights in using her business as a vehicle to support meaningful causes and organizations. To date, sales of Eytan's work have already helped to provide over twelve thousand nutritious meals to malnourished children overseas, and his artwork has been displayed by organizations that support research for autism. Looking toward the future, Susan, age fifty-four, jokes that she has so many ideas for growing the business and spreading Eytan's messages of inclusion and acceptance that she expects to work well into her eighties in order to make them all a reality!

Three Additional Insights from Socially Minded Entrepreneurs

1. "Don't be so in love with your original idea that you fail to see what else is out there. If you keep banging your head against the wall, you need to go in a different direction. The people that are successful are the ones that are willing to tweak things as they go along." —Anita Mahaffey

2. "When I've had success in something, it's normally something I really didn't slave away for and get; it's like the right moment came. I often think of the Shakespeare quote, 'There is a tide in the affairs of men.' You can do all the background work, but if the timing isn't right, none of it will come to fruition. Don't try to force it. Wait and let it all come together." —Dewey Crepeau, J.D.

3. "Starting something new in my fifties was a little scary and intimidating because I knew I'd have to use a lot of the new technology and I didn't know much about any of it. I had never created a website, didn't even know what a blog was, or what a tweet looked like, or how to use Facebook. But I was highly motivated by sharing Eytan's art and by the messages about respecting differences, so I concluded that I had to follow my intuition and trust that I would learn what I needed to learn." —Susan Nisinzweig

WORK FOR A BUSINESS WITH A CONSCIENCE

Finally, this last idea is for those of you who want to continue working within your industry, but in a more socially conscious manner. Idealist.org, an outstanding site for people interested in socially responsible careers, suggests that job seekers can enter into a business career with social impact through three different paths:

1. You can find a position focused on corporate responsibility and sustainability within a for-profit entity.

2. You can secure employment with a socially responsible company that values the triple-bottom-line approach (people, planet, and profits) as a core value in their business.

3. You can focus on opportunities within an industry sector that is focused on social responsibility goals.

For example, if you used to work for an oil company, you might want to now work for a company focused on renewable energy; if you used to work in commercial banking, you might want to shift into microfinance. Figuring out just the right way to leverage these strategies within your industry will take a bit of research. Here are three suggestions to help you make the shift:

1. Take a look at the socially responsible–oriented courses that are now being offered to professionals in your industry. You may be surprised to discover that the range of options has changed considerably since you were a student. Check with your industry association (industry journals and magazines often have articles about emerging trends) to learn about new certifications and classes that will help you gain the needed credentials to specialize in a more socially responsible niche.

2. Several of this country's leading universities—including Harvard, Duke, Stanford, and Dartmouth—have developed innovative programs in social entrepreneurship, sustainability, and microfinance. Reading about their programs will educate you about the range of ways you might be able to use your skills to make a difference in the for-profit arena.

3. Community colleges and trade schools are offering an increasing number of certificate and credentialing programs that have a socially conscious focus. For example, many design schools are now offering classes in green design and community colleges are training people in the skills needed to address climate change, environmental stewardship, and the green workforce.

Here are some additional resources to help you find information and listings about socially responsible jobs:

- **Justmeans (www.justmeans.com).** This site is an excellent source of information about sustainability and social enterprise.

- **Ethical Performance (www.ethicalperformance.com).** This website focuses on corporate social responsibility and socially responsible investment.

- **Green America (www.greenbusinessnetwork.org).** This site has information about thousands of companies that are committed to working in a more environmentally responsible way.

THREE FINAL THOUGHTS ON MAKING A LIVING WHILE MAKING A DIFFERENCE

1. **Don't believe the myths about working for nonprofits.** Blanket statements like "You won't earn any money" or "Nonprofits are frustrating places to work" are simply unfounded. Organizations are as diverse as the people who run them. Do your homework, find a good fit, and actively tune out the doubters.

2. **Money matters.** Nonprofits look for people with a wide variety of skills. But if you are adept at fund-raising, development, or writing grants, you are going to be a particularly attractive candidate in the nonprofit world. People who can bring funds into organizations are always in demand.

3. **Commit to action.** Whether you choose to work for a nonprofit, act as a socially conscious entrepreneur, or focus on a more socially responsible way to work in your industry, remember that the paths to doing good works are limitless, but the time to act is not. As we conclude this chapter, it's helpful to reflect on these words from the late great Arthur Ashe: "From what we get, we can make a living; what we give, however, can make a life."

Folsom

****

Gilberti, Nancy C

Wed Jun 14 2017

Second-act careers : 50+ ways to

33029097377527

*

*

*

*

*

*

*

06/23/2017

Gilberti, Nancy C

CHAPTER SEVEN

Get Paid to Travel

Okay, I'll admit that I saved the most fun category of second-act careers for last. And, I suspect that more than one of you skipped over the preceding chapters so you could read this one first! Indeed, the prospect of getting paid to travel is enticing, especially when you're at a point in life that you already plan to do a lot of travel, regardless of the costs involved. Although the idea of being compensated for travel may sound like a fantasy, the reality is that it *can* happen, but the amount you get paid will depend on a number of variables. In some cases, you will be paid a fee for your services; in other situations, you'll receive "in-kind" compensation (free lodging, meals, and so on) that will offset the costs associated with your travels.

Please keep your expectations in check and know that none of the options in this chapter are going to earn you a fortune. But they might significantly enrich your world by enabling you to travel more frequently, visit places you otherwise could not afford, and enjoy one-of-a-kind immersion travel experiences—all without having to dip into your savings account. If that strikes you as a priceless combination, I think you'll find this chapter an especially appealing read.

TOUR DIRECTOR

How would you like to get paid for leading tours in beautiful places? Tour directors are hired by tour companies to lead groups of people on multiday excursions throughout the world. It is not only a fun job, but it is also a job that appears to have strong growth potential; more than eighty million Americans travel on group tours annually, and as the baby boomers enter their retirement years, those numbers are likely to increase significantly. As a tour director, you'll be responsible for keeping your charges entertained, engaged, and on schedule while you lead the group from place to place. In some parts of the world, tour directors must be professionally certified, licensed, or both before being allowed to work, but certification is generally not required in the States. The following interview will help you learn about this intriguing career.

INTERVIEW WITH THE TOUR DIRECTOR EXPERT

"It's a vocation, not a vacation. But it's the best job in the world as far as I am concerned."

—FRANK M. SLATER, CEO and owner of International Guide Academy

What types of characteristics are important for success as a tour director?

F.S: This job is for a people person: someone who is outgoing and energetic and enjoys educating others. Hopefully you are the type of person who never tires of travel; you'll be as awed by the Grand Canyon the tenth time you see it as you were the first.

Is this job a good fit for people over fifty?

F.S: No question! This is a profession that is "age insensitive." It may be one of the few jobs where age is an advantage—people tend to like having a more "mature" person leading the groups, especially when the group consists of people who are seniors themselves.

How much are tour directors paid?

F.S: As a tour director, you can expect to earn an average of about $3,000 in wages, tips, and commissions over the course of a ten-day assignment. In addition, all your travel costs will be covered; you'll get to enjoy the same hotels, dining experiences, and outings as your group. That means if you go on a trip valued at $8,000, and you get paid $3,000 in wages, your total compensation will be roughly equal to $11,000—not bad for ten days worth of work!

What are the some of the challenges of being a tour director?

F.S: It can be tiring. You need to be comfortable with the idea of being away from home for weeks at a time. As the person in charge, you have to be ready to respond calmly when things don't go according to plan. The unexpected happens: people get sick, planes get delayed, hotels lose reservations, and buses break down. Most of the time trips run smoothly, but it helps if you're the type of person who doesn't get flustered easily.

Can spouses travel along?

F.S: Yes, most of the time. Some companies will allow your spouse to travel along for free (a rarity), but even if they need to pay for their trip, their room will be free because you will be sharing accommodations.

Can people do this on a part-time basis?

F.S: Most people work part-time. You can work as much or as little as you want, within reason. Of course, if you only make yourself available for a few weeks a year, you won't be as in demand as someone who works six months out of the year. But if you only want to run tours during leaf-season in New England (or some other seasonal event), it is possible to work that way.

What trends do you see that might impact this opportunity?

F.S: Women-only tours, ecotourism, and adventure tours are some of the fastest-growing niches in the tour industry.

For more information, consult these resources:

- The International Guide Academy (www.bepaidtotravel.com)
- International Tour Management Institute (www.itmitourtraining.com)
- Local colleges, for tour guide training programs

TOUR GUIDES

If you like the idea of leading tours but don't want to have to do the overnight trips associated with being a tour director, you might prefer to work as a local tour guide. Private tour companies, conventions, and tourist bureaus hire tour guides to lead groups on visits to national parks, historic neighborhoods, famous sites, and scenic places. Like tour directors, tour guides can work part-time or year-round, although most guides work on a part-time basis. As a tour guide, you can earn an average of $20 to $50 per hour (bilingual guides can command up to $75 per hour).

The variety of tours being offered is growing all the time. These days you can find food tours, ghost tours, tours that cater to grandparents, and tours unique to a specific locale, such as A Slice of Brooklyn Pizza Tours in Brooklyn, New York, or the Savannah Historic Homes Walk offered in Savannah, Georgia. If you live in a major city or tourist area, you may be able to create a specialty tour of your own that you market through hotels, convention services, and other tourist attractions. Tour guides are generally trained on the job, but many people obtain additional training through certificate programs offered by tourism schools and community colleges. Although it is not always necessary to be certified, you can earn a Certified Tour Professional (CTP) certification through the National Tour Association (NTA) (www.ntaonline.com).

To learn more:

- International Guide Academy (www.bepaidtotravel.com)

- International Tour Management Institute (www.itmitourtraining
  .com)

- Food Tour Pros, for guidance in creating a food tour or culinary
  tour in your city (www.foodtourpros.com)

Associations can also be a good source of information about training, jobs, and employers. Here is a sampling of tour guide associations located in different cities:

- Chicago: www.tourguidesofchicago.com

- Dallas/Fort Worth: www.dfwtourguides.com

- New Orleans: www.nolatourguides.org

- New York: www.ganyc.org

- San Diego: sdtourguides.com

START AN IMPORT-EXPORT BUSINESS

When I travel, I love nothing more than to spend time meandering in and out of the local shops, browsing street vendors and neighborhood markets in search of unique and unusual native products. But until I did research for this book, I never realized that I could use that shopping as a way to generate a positive cash flow.

As it turns out, there is good money to be earned from importing high-demand products like artisanal foods, furniture, and unique crafts. According to the US Small Business Administration, you can command margins of up to 700 percent for certain items. Of course, before you get involved with any type of importing activity, you should research US trade barriers and local in-country laws to be sure that you can legally export your goods out of the country and into the United

States. There are safety, quality, and environmental controls that may also impact your importing activities, and you may need a license or permit before importing certain goods.

To help you learn more about this career option, I turned to Alison Talbert of Wilmington, North Carolina, who found a second-act career as an importer and recently developed both an online training program and a "group buying trip" for people interested in learning how to make a business out of importing goods from Ecuador.

Getting Paid to Shop

"If you have a passion for travel and love beautiful things, this is a wonderful business."
—Alison Talbert, founder of Income from Ecuador (www.incomefromecuador.com)

Several years ago Alison Talbert, a former travel agent turned stay-at-home mom, was itching to go back to work. But with two teens still living at home, she didn't want to return to work on a full-time basis. After considering a variety of options, Alison learned about a course for people interested in importing goods from Ecuador. Intrigued by the idea of a flexible job that would allow her to travel (and after consulting a map to learn where Ecuador was located!), Alison took off for a learning trip to Ecuador. As part of her training program, she had the opportunity to travel the countryside and meet with local artisans. She fell in love with the people and products of Ecuador; by the time she headed home, she had filled two suitcases with crafts, and her head was buzzing with business ideas.

Since that first visit, Alison, now age forty-five, has been back to Ecuador dozens of times. On each trip she buys new items—buttery leather bags, finely woven shawls, and one-of-a-kind jewelry pieces—that she sells to her growing list of clients back home. Over the years, she has developed a good understanding of what her clients look for, and she advises her vendors on the best ways to customize their products to maximize the sales of their goods. In addition to buying handicrafts, she now also imports roses and other flowers that she is able to sell at extremely competitive prices. Alison has plans to open an online retail store and is working with her vendors to prepare them to handle the additional orders.

What started as a fun way to make some extra money has slowly evolved into a more serious home-based business enterprise. But no matter how busy she gets, Alison continues to have a wonderful time shopping, exploring, and discovering new treasures to import. She is living her dream life and teaching others how to do the same. "I love to see when the lightbulb goes on and people realize that this is a real opportunity, not some pie-in-the-sky thing," says Allison. Perhaps most important, she feels great about helping her vendors in Ecuador prosper. Knowing that her business helps them to earn a good living and provide a better life for their families is immensely rewarding. "The people are so lovely and sweet," says Alison. "Every time I place an order, it helps them. And, for me, that's the best part of the business."

Alison's Top Three Tips for the Import Business

1. **There are many ways to sell your goods.** You can sell at home parties, crafts fairs, boutiques, and festivals. You could also sell the items online, either through your own website or by listing your goods with an online marketplace like Etsy.com or eBay.com.

2. **Consult high-end travel magazines.** *International Living* (www .internationalliving-magazine.com), for example, offers helpful information and articles about retirement living and business opportunities in different countries.

3. **Consider taking a course about importing goods from the country where you intend to operate.** To find an appropriate course, talk to people for recommendations, Google "export training course," and check the advertisements listed in travel magazines.

To learn more, consult the SBA website at www.sba.gov/content/ importing-goods for links to a number of helpful resources.

INNSITTERS

If you've ever dreamed about running your own bed and breakfast, but you don't want to be tied down to the business 24-7, you may be excited to learn about a career as an innsitter. As the name implies, innsitters work on a temporary basis, filling in for short periods of time while the inn's owners are away from the property. While on the job, you'll be the person in charge, with responsibility for ensuring the safety, comfort, and enjoyment of the guests. (You will typically spend at least a day with the innkeeper to learn the routine and procedures before the owner leaves the premises.) You'll cook omelets, schmooze with the guests, serve wine and cheese, and otherwise be the "hostess with the mostest." But once your assignment is completed, you are free to leave—and then you can return to your nice quiet home.

People who stay at inns expect to enjoy top-notch, personal service and attention to detail, so you need to be willing to work hard, be cheerful, and go the extra mile for your guests. For the right personality, it's a nice way to indulge your innkeeper fantasies, earn some extra income, and enjoy the chance to travel to different locales, without having to commit to the innkeeper's life full time. And if you think you might want to buy an inn at some point, working as an innsitter is a smart way to put that to the test and learn the business before investing in an inn of your own.

To learn more: There are numerous training courses and associations that can help you educate yourself about this career option. Here are three to get you started:

- Interim Innkeepers Network (www.interiminnkeepers.net)

- Inn Caring (training classes and seminars) (www.inncaring.com)

- Professional Association of Innkeepers International (www.innkeeping.org)

PROPERTY CARETAKING

Do you remember that television show *Lifestyles of the Rich and Famous*, hosted by Robin Leach and featuring the opulent homes of celebrities, stars, and moguls? I spent hours watching the parade of mansions and thinking that it would be very cool to live in one of those houses, at least for a few days. As it turns out, there might just be a way to finally make my "champagne wishes and caviar dreams" come true—should I ever care to pursue work as a temporary caretaker.

Who hires caretakers? Owners of private homes, resorts, boats, and villas all hire caretakers to watch over their properties and homes in their absence; the bigger and more expensive the property, the more likely it is that a caretaker will be needed. As a caretaker, your job duties and compensation will vary considerably from situation to situation. Sometimes all that is needed is for someone to stay on the premises so that the house appears occupied. In other cases, you'll be asked to work quite hard; you could help run a farm, oversee a small resort, or be in charge of maintenance.

You will almost always be provided free lodging in exchange for your caretaking services. In addition, you might be compensated in the form of meals, a salary, and even access to the family's swimming pool, tennis courts, cars, and other amenities. In general, caretaking jobs that involve more extensive responsibilities are compensated more generously than "stay and sleep" situations. You will probably have ample free time while you are "in residence," so this can be a fabulous arrangement if you're looking to live rent-free in a beautiful location, while you spend time pursuing other interests like writing, painting, or developing your own internet-based business.

To learn more about caretaking opportunities, consult the Caretaking Gazette (www.caretaker.org), a website and newsletter that lists caretaking jobs worldwide. Trusted Housesitters is another good resource at www.trustedhousesitters.com.

VOLUNTEER VACATIONS

How would you like the chance to blend travel with the opportunity to make the world a better place? If that sounds like a worthy goal, you may want to consider signing up for a volunteer vacation. As you may suspect from the use of the word "volunteer," it is unusual to actually be *paid* to take a volunteer vacation. In fact, in the majority of cases, you will incur some costs to pay for these trips. Nonetheless, volunteer vacations provide a meaningful and unique way to indulge your love of travel, at a fraction of the cost of a more conventional vacation. If you plan on doing a lot of travel in retirement, this is a wonderful way to do it for pennies on the dollar. (You may be able to further defray the costs of your travel if your church, synagogue, or local volunteer organization is willing to sponsor your efforts as part of their charitable outreach initiatives). And there are some exceptions to the "no-pay" rule—in some cases you will be paid a small stipend for your volunteer services. Paid or not, these trips can truly be a once-in-a-lifetime experience that will enrich your life and nourish your soul in a way that few other trips ever will. To help you learn more about this option, I interviewed Sheryl Kane, an expert on immersion travel, who recently wrote two books on this topic.

ADVICE FROM THE VOLUNTEER VACATION EXPERT

"Stipends and internships are no longer just for the young."
—SHERYL KAYNE, author

When Sheryl Kayne thought about writing a book about volunteer vacations, she was surprised to discover that all the available books on the subject focused on international volunteer opportunities. Sheryl knew that there were hundreds of volunteer opportunities in the United States, so she decided to write two books, *Immersion Travel USA* (Countryman Press, 2008) and *Volunteer*

Vacations across America (Chicago Review Press, 2009) that highlight those domestic opportunities. The best way to appreciate the full range of options is to read her books, but for now, here is a small sampling of possibilities:

- **Casting for Recovery (castingforrecovery.org).** This nonprofit provides fly-fishing retreats for women who have or have had breast cancer. They look for volunteers with fly-fishing experience, psychotherapists with experience leading group sessions, and people willing to act as retreat leaders and helpers. The program is free for volunteers, but you will need to pay the costs of your transportation to and from the retreat locations.

- **Jackson Hole Film Festival (jacksonholefilminstitute.org).** If you have a passion for both the arts and nature, consider spending a week in beautiful Jackson Hole, Wyoming, working at a film festival that advances the art of independent films. Although you'll have to pay for your own transportation and housing, if you volunteer for over twelve hours, you'll get a free five-day cinema pass, free food, and an insider's peek into this exciting event.

- **Wolf Rescue, Wild Spirit Wolf Sanctuary (www.wildspirit wolfsanctuary.org).** The wolf sanctuary rescues abused and abandoned wolves and provides educational services on this subject for the public. You must commit to work for at least two months or longer; in exchange, you'll be given housing, a food allotment, and (when funding allows) a small stipend.

- **Lighthouse keeper.** How would you like to live in a lighthouse rent-free? You can—in exchange for providing services such as facilitating tours and assisting park rangers. To find out more, check The Lighthouse News at www.lighthouse-news.com for news reports and job openings at lighthouses.

{continued}

- **National Park Service (NPS) (www.nps.gov).** Over one hundred thousand people volunteer at our national parks each year, and some of those volunteers get to live in the parks for free. For example, the artist-in-residence program provides an opportunity for visual artists, sculptors, performers, writers, composers, and other artists to live and work in the parks. Sheryl applied for the program as a writer and received free housing, a free pass to the Everglades National Park, and the opportunity to have plenty of time to devote to her writing.

Sheryl's Top Three Tips for Volunteer Vacationers

1. **Check references.** Ask for the opinions and suggestions of people who have previously gone on a volunteer vacation. You'll want to ensure that the living and working conditions are as good as promised.

2. **Look into tax breaks.** Many volunteer vacations qualify in part or wholly as a tax-deductible expense. (Be sure to check with the program staff and your tax adviser.)

3. **Just do it!** Volunteer vacations can be one of the least expensive but most meaningful vacation experiences of your life. You will return home a very different person from the one who left.

To learn more about domestic volunteer vacations, consult Sheryl's books or her site at www.immersiontraveler.com. For information about international volunteer vacations, try these resources:

- Globe Aware, a nonprofit that develops short-term volunteer programs in international environments (www.globeaware.org).

- Global Volunteers, an organization that hosts short- and long-term volunteer trips (www.globalvolunteers.org).

- Worldwide Opportunities on Organic Farms offers a list of different places where you can work on organic farms (www.wwoof.org).

JOBS IN COOL PLACES

As I hope you realize by now, there are all sorts of interesting ways to combine work and travel. Before concluding this chapter, here are three more ideas to ponder:

1. **The National Parks.** Our parks can't depend only on volunteers to run efficiently—they employ thousands of paid workers each summer as well. The range of jobs at the parks covers gift shop sales, administrative posts, and jobs as oral interpreters. There are ample opportunities for people with all sorts of skills and talents interested in temporary and seasonal positions. For example, Glacier National Park has a fleet of historic red buses that are driven by seasonally hired drivers who give oral histories of the park to visiting tourists. If you prefer sea to land, look into getting hired for a summer season as a boat captain by the Glacier Park Boat Company (www.glacierparkboats.com). To learn more about jobs in our parks, consult the park's official website at www.nps.gov.

2. **Cruise ships.** Cruise ships hire people to help feed, entertain, educate, and take care of their guests. Whether you want to work in the gift shop, bake in the kitchen, or sing in the theaters, there are opportunities to get paid to work at sea. Although the pay is generally a bit less than what you will be paid on land for the same work, your room and board will be covered. People who are "experts" can sometimes earn free cruises in exchange for giving lectures or teaching classes on the ship.

   To learn more, go to the careers page of any of the major cruise lines or consult the JobMonkeys.com page about careers on cruise ships at www.jobmonkey.com/cruise.

3. **Teaching English overseas.** Even in a weak global economy, the opportunities to teach English overseas are robust. In most instances, all you need to qualify for a teaching job is a bachelor's degree, but candidates with advanced training and either a certificate in English as a Second Language (ESL) or a master's degree in Teaching English to Speakers of Other Languages (TESOL) enjoy greater job opportunities and earnings potential. Many programs require a minimum one-year commitment from job applicants. Earnings potential can range from a small living stipend to $50,000 or more depending on your expertise and location. As an added bonus, your income may be exempt from federal and/or state taxes if you meet the qualifications for the foreign earned income exemption.

To learn more, consult the Teach English as a Foreign Language database at www.tefl.net/tefl-courses/index.htm; TransitionsAbroad .com has listings for teaching jobs as well as other listings of overseas employment (www.transitionsabroad.com).

THREE FINAL TIPS ON GETTING PAID TO TRAVEL

1. **Learn more.** There are many more ways to get paid to travel than I had space for in this chapter. Take the time to read some of the many great books that are available on this topic. One particularly helpful resource is *Work Your Way Around the World* by Susan Griffiths (Crimson Publishing, 14th edition, 2009).

2. **Get creative.** It is easy to get lured into the luxury travel ideal perpetuated by the tourism industry. But with just a little bit of creativity and a willingness to forgo fancy golf courses and chocolate on your pillows (at least some of the time), you can significantly reduce your travel expenses and enjoy top travel destinations at a fraction of the cost of a

conventional vacation. Living in a cabin while working in the national parks or working on an organic farm can be just as rejuvenating as relaxing in a spa at a luxury hotel.

3. **Think like a teenager.** As I write this, my daughter has just left for a semester of study abroad in Copenhagen. This isn't her first trip out of the country. At the ripe old age of twenty-one, she has already done two service trips: one helping to build a school in Costa Rica and the other working on an organic farm in Puerto Rico. Our children have grown up in a world where immersion travel and volunteer vacations are no longer an exotic option. They are using the Internet to find rewarding ways to travel and organizations willing to help fund their trips. They aren't waiting until they can afford the Ritz-Carlton, and neither should we. There is literally a world of options for adventure travel—you just have to be willing to loosen up and let go of your preconceptions of what con-stitutes a great travel experience.

CHAPTER EIGHT

Ten Reinvention Lessons Learned

Before we move on to the next part of this book, I want to take a moment to pause and consider the lessons learned from the people profiled thus far. Reflecting back on all the wonderful conversations I was privileged to have, I was impressed by how much each of them taught me about what it takes to have a successful career reinvention. Of course, in my job as a career coach, I get to see career reinvention in action all the time. But the reality is that when I coach clients, they are "works in progress," and their stories can take months and sometimes even years to unfold. Writing this book gave me a very different perspective, as I listened to dozens of success stories—from start to finish—in rapid-fire succession. There was one week in particular in which I conducted nearly twenty interviews, and although the details of each story were as unique as the personalities involved, I couldn't help but notice that I was hearing certain underlying themes repeated over and over again. Let's now take a closer look at those lessons learned:

1. **Let go to grow.** All too many of us fall into the trap of allowing society to define success for us. But knowing and claiming what you *really* want, as opposed to what society claims you *should* want, is a critical link to success in the reinvention process. When you're willing to let go of the glossy trappings of your career in favor of more personally significant paths, amazing transformations can and will happen. Of course, saying it and doing it are two different things, and letting go of old identities isn't easy, especially when you've spent years working hard to establish yourself in your professional life. But one of the commonalities I noticed among the people I interviewed was their willingness to trade in their old "acceptable" titles for newer "riskier" roles. Bob Alper, the rabbi turned stand-up comedian; Eve Young, the mom and volunteer turned acting extra; and Dewey Crepeau, the attorney turned adoption agency owner—all took that risk, and it paid off handsomely. I love it when Eve says of her decision to pursue acting: "I finally realized the only person stopping me, was me."

2. **Recognize that adversity can lead to opportunity.** Many of the people profiled in this book weren't necessarily looking to change their careers. But a significant number of them were forced to do so in response to the financial crisis of 2008. (I was amazed by the number of times I typed some version of the phrase "and then in 2008 . . .") They succeeded in part because they chose to interpret the turbulence in their lives as an opportunity instead of an obstacle. Once they got over the initial shock of their new reality, they decided to view the fork in the road as a fresh start. It wasn't fun or easy, but their willingness to reframe adversity into a potential advantage allowed them to explore options that they might not have previously considered.

3. **Plan for serendipity.** I realize that is an oxymoron; you can't plan where, when, or how serendipity will happen. But as the Roman philosopher Seneca wrote, "Luck is what happens when preparation meets opportunity." The people profiled in this book seem

to intuitively understand this, and they consistently act accordingly. They make it a point to speak to strangers. They ask a lot of questions. They join clubs, participate in professional groups, and get involved with their communities. When presented with an opportunity, their default response is to ask "why not?" instead of "why?" And as a result, they "get lucky." Take a page from their playbook: the next time someone extends an invitation, accept it; the next time you hesitate to try something new, gulp and go for it; and the next time you're sitting next to someone on an airplane, start a conversation and see where it leads. If you do, you might just find your new attitude will lead to a world of "lucky" career options and unexpected good fortune.

4. **Adopt an opportunity-seeker mind-set.** Never before in history have we enjoyed easier access to more information. Every day we have the opportunity to learn about thousands, even millions, of new ideas and possibilities from newspapers, television, and the Internet. You can make it a point to consciously pay attention to this information, or you can choose to ignore it. Many of the people profiled in this book found their second-act opportunities simply by keeping their "opportunity antenna" on alert and paying closer attention to what they were reading. Joanne Schumacher, the VP profiled in chapter five, discovered her flexible job one morning while browsing through an e-mail newsletter. She wasn't actively looking for a job, but she took the time to interview, and it led to a wonderful opportunity. Eve Young read an article about the Celebrant Foundation in her local newspaper, and that story resulted in her new career as a life-cycle celebrant. Beth Chapman, the senior move manager profiled in chapter three, learned about her new career though a newspaper article a friend sent her. Opportunity is everywhere. But you have to be alert enough to recognize it, take the time to consider it, and then be willing to act on it.

5. **Attitude trumps ability.** The people I interviewed for this book represent a wide range of talent, ability, and backgrounds. But there was one characteristic that they appeared to share in common: a healthy optimism and can-do spirit. It's no wonder. A positive outlook enables people to more easily try new challenges and situations, and that, in turn, leads to a higher rate of success. As hockey great Wayne Gretzky once famously said, "You miss 100 percent of the shots you don't take." Maintaining a positive outlook is not always easy (and there is no question that some people are naturally more optimistic than others), but simply being aware of your attitude, and making small adjustments when possible, is a good first step toward creating a more positive mindset. Make it a habit to adopt behaviors that have been proven to enhance well-being: surround yourself with a strong support team, exercise on a daily basis, get out in the sunshine, develop an attitude of gratitude, and limit your daily intake of negative media. You'll be surprised at how effectively—and easily—those behavioral habits will enhance the upward trajectory of your reinvention journey.

6. **Appreciate your age as an advantage.** We are all too familiar with the problems of age—the graying hair, bulging belly, failing eyesight, and aching back. And there is no question that age discrimination is alive and well in the workplace. But if you choose your career options wisely, age doesn't have to be a negative. The second half of life should be a time to reap the benefits of the wisdom gained from your many years of learning, working, and traveling. Terri Lloyd, the cofounder of the Haggus Society, says, "I realize now that in my twenties and thirties I didn't have the maturity or the chops to succeed. If I had been successful then, I worry that I would have squandered that success." I heard that same sentiment repeated by other people in different ways. Susan Nisinzweig, founder of Eytan Art, says that she hopes to work until she is eighty so she'll have enough time to put all of her

ideas into action. Other people talked about the benefits of finally being freed up from the worries associated with raising a family, paying the mortgage, and climbing the corporate ladder. Choosing to focus on the very real benefits of this life stage will enable you to explore opportunities that might have been closed off to you at a younger age.

7. **Change is a constant, so embrace it.** We live in a world where the traditional formulas for business success have been turned upside down by the unpredictable forces of an internet-based global economy. "We're throwing spaghetti against the wall to see what sticks," says business coach, author, and speaker Jane Pollak. "Boiling that water. Dropping in the pasta. Tossing it at the wall. Noticing what happens, then rinsing and repeating. This is the new normal." That unrelenting change is both scary and intimidating, particularly for boomers used to a more struc-tured workplace. But the people I interviewed showed an unusual willingness to adapt their career plans and business models to changing circumstances. They embraced technology and learned how to leverage tools like blogs, digital downloads, and video to advance their businesses. There are no hard and fast rules in this rapidly evolving economy, but a willingness to adapt and continu-ally learn new technologies will be critical for success in virtually every career-related endeavor.

8. **Perseverance pays off.** Success isn't the result of one isolated decision, action, or event. It is the small actions you take each day that add up to big change over the course of the years. Each step builds on the next, and true progress comes from the les-sons and insights gained with every choice you make. Terri Lloyd says, "It isn't like a firecracker that goes off and suddenly you are catapulted. It is many, many small steps, lots of failures, and the accumulation of the learning along the way. All roads lead to someplace. Everything I've learned in my life has contributed to this moment." Terri is right. Don't expect overnight success.

Be patient, have confidence in your abilities, and trust that with time, your smaller steps will lead to larger triumphs.

9. **Fear is inevitable, but you can overcome it.** No matter how old we get, fear plays a role in our lives. But as I once heard a therapist explain, sometimes FEAR is just an acronym for "False Evidence Appearing Real." The people profiled in this book are no different from the rest of us; they all expressed some level of fear and insecurity. What made them different is that they didn't let their fears dictate their choices. They succeeded in spite of their concerns, by building on their strengths, minimizing unnecessary risks, and keeping themselves focused on what they could control and change.

10. **Education is the single best antidote for fear.** One of the best ways to conquer fear as you transition into your second-act career is with education and training. A great example of the power of education comes from Linda Pond, a fifty-five-year-old Canadian who, with the help of her daughter, invented the FAB light (FAB stands for "Find a Beer"), a nifty little lighting gadget that sticks to the inside lid of a camping cooler (www.lindaleepond.com). Linda had no prior experience with product invention, but over time she learned—now major retailers throughout North America sell the FAB light. She self-published a book about the adventure, called *Top Secrets of a Girl Entrepreneur*, and the publication of that book helped launch her career as a public speaker. Interestingly Linda says that until she was in her mid-forties, she often lacked confidence in her abilities. But once she recognized that the best way to deal with her insecurities was by getting training and experience, then she began to enjoy a steady stream of successes. As she gained confidence in her professional life, she became bolder in her personal life as well. She decided to try her hand at acting and landed a part in a local theater production. Then her goal became to both act and sing, and she did that too. Each success led to the next, and over time, she saw that she was

far more capable then she had previously believed. The same is true for many of the people I interviewed. Their willingness to try new things and invest in lifelong learning helped them overcome obstacles and be more successful in their second-act journeys.

They did it—and you can too. And I can think of no better way to illustrate this point than with this next and final profile.

From Cop to Comedian: A Lesson in Arresting Fear

"I'm getting pretty far in comedy. I have such a passion for it and I think when you have a passion, things just happen naturally."
—Gina Scarda, stand-up comic and actress

Gina Scarda's first career didn't take place anywhere near a stage, but it certainly involved more than its fair share of human drama. Back then her stage was the streets of New York, and her costars were pimps, murderers, and little old ladies in need of assistance. You see, Gina earned her living not as a performer but as a policewoman with the famed New York City Police Department. She began her career patrolling the streets of Coney Island and says she loved every minute of it. Whether she was doing quality-of-life sweeps ("you know, things like prostitution, underage drinking sweeps, anything that affects the quality of life in the neighborhood") or just talking with the people on the streets, life as a cop was a surprisingly fun fit. "Probably the best time in my life was when I started as a young cop," says Gina. "I had such a great time."

At age forty-six, after twenty years of service on the force, Gina retired with a full pension and benefits, right around the same time that her daughter, who had been active in theater in high school, was heading off to college. Gina hoped that her daughter would continue to pursue theatre in college ("I mean, what parent actually wants that for her daughter?" jokes Gina). But like most kids, her daughter had other plans, and she ultimately decided to focus on the sciences instead. Gina was disappointed by her daughter's decision, but when she made her sentiments known, her daughter responded by saying, "Mom, if you are so disappointed, why don't *you* go and become an actress yourself?"

Gina readily admits that she didn't even know that she harbored a passion for acting until her daughter pointed it out. But her daughter's challenge gave Gina just the nudge she needed to acknowledge both her hidden passion—and her hidden fears. Looking back on that conversation, Gina laughs as she acknowledges the irony in the situation. "You would think I would be braver. After all, I was a cop! But I guess the fear of failure kept me from doing it. Rejection is a horrible thing." After recognizing the fear, Gina decided the best way to conquer her nerves would be to get some training. She enrolled in a comedy class, and from the minute she walked on the stage, she felt like she was at home. A few months after taking her first class, she entered a contest for Long Island's Funniest Comedian and, much to her surprise, won the top prize. "That really helped boost my confidence," she says.

With her newfound self-assurance, Gina began to audition at open-mic nights at New York comedy clubs, a process that allowed her to try out new material and create a routine. Then one day "out of the blue," she received a phone call from a woman who had seen Gina's comedy video posted on the Internet. The woman explained that she thought Gina would be a good fit for a comedy group called The Italian Chicks, and she asked her to send a headshot and bio for review. Gina was flattered, but instead of jumping on the opportunity, she did nothing. "I didn't have either an updated resume or a headshot, so I kind of ignored it," she says. "I guess it was the fear again."

Three months later the same woman called her back, and this time Gina decided to give it a try. "I guess she was desperate," recalls Gina with a chuckle. "I freaked out a little, but I went and did it, and the minute I met the other girls in the act, I knew it was going to work. We connected immediately." The group started out doing dinner theatre pieces for fifty people and quickly built a following. They now travel all over the country and perform in front of audiences of five hundred people or more. At the same time that Gina works on her comedy, she continues to pursue more serious acting opportunities. In addition to working as an acting extra, she has done some small student films and commercial work. The week we spoke, she had just received her Screen Actors Guild

(SAG) card, an accomplishment that she admitted brought tears to her eyes ("I must be menopausal," she jokes).

Gina is amazed at the great luck she has enjoyed since she "retired." She is quick to credit her husband for supporting and encouraging her along the way. And even though her children are still a bit mortified by her act (her seventeen-year-old son refuses to come to her shows), she knows they have been inspired by both her success and her willingness to conquer her fears. "It's been such a great influence on my children to have them see me going after my dreams," says Gina. "For the longest time, I felt guilty about doing something for myself. But they love it. It shows them that they can do anything. I want them to know they can have dreams too."

Gina's Top Three Tips for Aspiring Comics and Actors

1. **Be willing to take on small jobs.** Gina says that her experiences working as an extra on movie and television sets have provided invaluable networking opportunities that she knows will lead to better opportunities over time.

2. **Don't assume you need to live in New York to pursue acting.** You don't need to be in New York or Los Angeles to do this type of work (although it helps). There are acting jobs in many other cities. For people in the New York tri-state area, Gina recommends NYCastings.com.

3. **Take baby steps toward success.** Start with a class to see whether you like performing in front of an audience. If you can't get up in front of a small class and perform, then this isn't for you. Build up your audiences slowly. You start with six people, which turns into fifty people, which turns into an audience of hundreds. Bit by bit, you'll grow more comfortable and confident.

PART TWO

Creating Your Second-Act Career

Are you feeling energized, excited, and hopeful about the possibilities for your second-act career? I certainly hope so! After all, as you discovered from reading the stories in part one, it's not just a second act; it's a second chance! But as enticing as that sounds, I suspect that right about now many of you are also feeling a bit uncertain about your own next steps. *How do I get started? What should I be focused on? What are my best options?* This section of the book will help you answer those questions, and others, as you build the road map for your own second act.

As we go along, you'll discover that planning for your semi-retirement career is a somewhat different process from your previous career transitions. When you think back to the last time you planned your career (junior year in college?), it's likely that your decisions were based more on practical concerns, like paying the rent and putting food on the table, than on your personal hopes and dreams. But now it is time to switch things up. Instead of allowing your career to dominate your life, it's time for your life to take center stage. This is a welcome opportunity to make time for travel, to learn a new language or work for a meaningful cause; the freedom to explore new interests, take calculated risks, and stretch beyond your comfort zone; and a chance to live a more balanced life, with time for exercising, reading, playing golf, or visits with the grandchildren.

In this section, I am going to walk you through a five-step process designed to help you gain clarity about the type of life—and the type of work—that you want to pursue during your semi-retirement. As you work through the steps, you'll be answering a variety of questions intended to help you better understand your motivating interests, skills, and drivers. There are many methodologies for reassessing our careers: assessments, quizzes, and the like. Ultimately, however, my professional experience has taught me that there is no better way to understand yourself than good old-fashioned self-reflection. After all, *you* are the only person who actually knows what you really want. The exercises in this section will help you gain a better understanding of what that is.

HOW TO USE THIS SECTION

Work through the exercises at your own pace and come back and revise them as necessary. But do try to start this sooner rather than later. The speed of the reinvention process varies from person to person; some people find quick gratification, whereas others slowly build toward success. Allow enough space for the process to unfold and evolve without unneeded pressure.

I encourage you to use a separate notebook (or computer file) to record your thoughts as you work through these exercises (there is some space provided in the book, but you will likely need more). Whichever method you choose, please be sure to write down your answers to the questions in this section. Capturing your ideas on paper (or on your computer) is always more effective than keeping your thoughts locked up inside your head. Writing them down will also create a permanent record of your thoughts for future reference. Finally, you may also find it beneficial to discuss the results of your exercises with friends or family—sharing your thoughts with others will help to both clarify your thinking and provide needed encouragement and support along your reinvention journey.

CHAPTER NINE
Envision the Life You Want

When you are freed up from *having* to work a traditional nine-to-five job, the options for how, when, and where you might *choose* to work expand exponentially. But choosing from that world of possibilities can feel downright overwhelming. So, before figuring out the career piece of the semi-retirement puzzle, it's helpful to spend some time clarifying your lifestyle goals: How many hours do you want to work? Do you want to run your own business? What type of balance do you want to strike between work, family, community, play, and self?

This first exercise will help you to develop a vision of your ideal semi-retirement lifestyle—not the "let's take off for the Bahamas and drink rum punches all day" type of ideal, but a life you see yourself happily living day after day. You want a vision that makes you think, "This works. I can see myself doing this. It feels right." Once you've defined the type of life you want to lead, it will be far easier to focus in on the types of businesses, income streams, and jobs that will best support your lifestyle.

EXERCISE: VISUALIZE YOUR IDEAL LIFE

Instructions: Close your eyes, quiet your mind, and try to picture what your day will be like when you are semi-retired. Visualize yourself as you go through the day. Make note of the details: the time you get out of bed, what you eat for breakfast, and the clothes you are wearing. Picture yourself as you go about your day and notice your surroundings. Who are you with? What types of activities are you involved in? Do you take time for lunch with a friend or indulge in a midday siesta? Are you taking classes or reading or listening to music? What do you eat for dinner? What do you talk about over dinner? How do you wrap up the day?

Open your eyes. What did you "see" during your ideal day? Think about what jumped out at you, surprised you, and impressed you. Now, while that vision is fresh in your mind, please answer the following questions:

- What activities and experiences do you want to make more time for in your life? This can include "big" items like travel or simple things like having time to make a nutritious dinner every night. Don't forget to include personal development priorities like spiritual growth, personal relationships, intellectual development, community involvement, cultural enrichment, or fitness goals.

- What type of schedule is going to work for your second act? Are you interested in seasonal employment, part-time work, work-from-home jobs, or simply having more control over your work schedule? Do you want summers off or evenings free?

- Do you want to work for someone else or be self-employed?

- What type of work setting appeals to you?

- What types of people do you want to work with or around?

- What topics, issues, or ideas do you want to incorporate into your day?

Write down a summary of your "Ideal Life Vision" below:

_____

_____

_____

_____

_____

_____

_____

Now that your mind is focused on the type of lifestyle you want, the next exercise will help you gain additional clarity about your key motivators and drivers. In other words, what is going to make you want to jump out of bed and enjoy your work and life each day?

EXERCISE: DISCOVER YOUR PERSONAL MOTIVATORS

As you review your ideal life vision, think about what you really value or need in your work life: What motivates you to get up in the morning? Which job duties, work missions, and environments make you love your work? There are so many things you could do, but knowing what is most important to you in this next phase of your life will make it much easier to focus in on opportunities that really feed your soul.

Instructions: The following are work-related needs and values. Thinking about what you want for this next stage in your life (not what you may have chosen in the past), please rank them on a continuum of one to five (one is not important, three is neutral, five is extremely important):

Achievement: Have opportunities to excel and produce significant results

1 —————— 2 —————— 3 —————— 4 —————— 5

Adventure: Do work that involves risk and allows for frequent new experiences

1 —————— 2 —————— 3 —————— 4 —————— 5

Aesthetics: Be involved with work that involves beautiful things and settings

1 —————— 2 —————— 3 —————— 4 —————— 5

Affiliation: Identify myself as an integral part of a group where I can develop close working relationships in pursuit of a common goal

1 —————— 2 —————— 3 —————— 4 —————— 5

Animals and Nature: Do work that allows me to spend time with animals and/or in nature

1 —————— 2 —————— 3 —————— 4 —————— 5

Autonomy: Work with little supervision and have control over my day-to-day activities

1 —————— 2 —————— 3 —————— 4 —————— 5

Artistic Expression: Engage in a creative and/or artistic endeavor

1 —————— 2 —————— 3 —————— 4 —————— 5

Builds on Experience: Get involved with work that builds on my professional experience and allows me to stay in my field of expertise

1 —————— 2 —————— 3 —————— 4 —————— 5

Community: Align with work that has a strong community component

1 —————— 2 —————— 3 —————— 4 —————5

Competition: Work in environments that encourage and reward competition

1 —————— 2 —————— 3 —————— 4 —————5

Cultural Diversity: Be involved in work that supports, promotes, or fosters cultural diversity and understanding

1 —————— 2 —————— 3 —————— 4 —————5

Ethics: Engage in work that is strongly in sync with my personal code of ethics

1 —————— 2 —————— 3 —————— 4 —————5

Fame: Do work that allows me to be recognized and lauded by my peers

1 —————— 2 —————— 3 —————— 4 —————5

Fun: Work in an environment that perpetually fosters fun, laughter, and play

1 —————— 2 —————— 3 —————— 4 —————5

Give Back: Be involved in work that easily allows me to give back to society

1 —————— 2 —————— 3 —————— 4 —————5

Influence: Be in a position of authority that allows me to affect how people think

1 —————— 2 —————— 3 —————— 4 —————5

Leadership: Do work that allows me to function as a leader of others

1 —————— 2 —————— 3 —————— 4 —————5

Mentorship: Be in a position that allows me to teach, coach, and inspire others

1 ——————— 2 ——————— 3 ——————— 4 ———————5

Nurturing Others: Participate in work that rewards me for nurturing others

1 ——————— 2 ——————— 3 ——————— 4 ———————5

Organization and Order: Do work that values order, systems, and planning

1 ——————— 2 ——————— 3 ——————— 4 ———————5

Power: Operate from a position of authority and have control over key decisions

1 ——————— 2 ——————— 3 ——————— 4 ———————5

Prestige: Work in a field that is considered very prestigious by society

1 ——————— 2 ——————— 3 ——————— 4 ———————5

Profit: Be responsible for impacting the bottom line

1 ——————— 2 ——————— 3 ——————— 4 ———————5

Public Exposure: Work in a field that allows me to frequently interact with the public

1 ——————— 2 ——————— 3 ——————— 4 ———————5

Stability: Work in a field that is considered stable and relatively "secure"

1 ——————— 2 ——————— 3 ——————— 4 ———————5

Travel: Do work that incorporates my love of travel

1 ——————— 2 ——————— 3 ——————— 4 ———————5

Instructions: Looking over your answers, what are the most important work-related motivators to look for in your second act? Write down your top ten motivators on this blank page.

THREE MORE WAYS TO VISUALIZE YOUR FUTURE

Visualization is a powerful and transformative tool for people looking to reinvent their careers. Expressing your career and life-style goals through pictures, as opposed to articulating them in words, can be a useful way to unlock vital clues and patterns that you may have been struggling to express using words alone. Here are three ways to use the power of images in your life to help supplement the exercises in this section:

1. **Keep a clippings file.** Do you sometimes clip articles and photos from magazines for a "dream" file of beautiful homes or vacation ideas? Do the same for your career. Collect pictures and articles that speak to you and capture your imagination. Don't be judgmental about what you choose to keep—with time you'll discover interesting commonalities and patterns among the items you have saved.

2. **Meditate.** Set aside some quiet time to meditate on the types of activities and work environment that would make you happy. Notice the images that come to mind. Do you prefer to be in a fast-paced office or a quiet one? Urban or rural settings? Are you happier being with lots of people or working in solitude? Look for patterns and themes in your mental images.

3. **Build a vision board.** A vision board is a collection of visual images (photos, memorabilia, pictures torn from maga-zines) displayed on a bulletin board or poster as a graphic representation of your dreams and ambitions. Once you've completed the board, display it in a prominent place as a visual reminder of your ambitions and career goals. If you're comfortable with technology, try using Pinterest.com, an online site where you can "pin" images from the Web to create virtual vision boards.

EXERCISE: WHAT *DON'T* YOU WANT?

One of the joys of planning a semi-retirement career is that you are finally at a point where you no longer have to do those things you really hate doing. Knowing what you want to avoid in your next career is as valuable as knowing what you want to include. Although every job or business is going to have some percentage of tasks that you are not happy about doing, the key is to focus on opportunities that minimize those negatives as much as possible.

Instructions: I'd like you to think about what you don't want to have to do anymore. Don't ever want to work a night shift again? Write it down. Tired of the stresses of running your own business? Make a note of that. Not interested in doing any more business travel? Okay then, put that down too. Make a thorough list of your pet peeves and then write down your top three here.

_____

_____

_____

EXERCISE: FINANCIAL VISION

This book is not intended to be a financial guide. That said, there are financial issues that must be taken into account when deciding on your vision for your semi-retirement, even if income is not a primary concern. At a minimum, you should have clear answers to the following questions:

- How much money do you need to earn?

- How much do you want to earn?

- Do you need to purchase health insurance?

- How much are you willing to invest in education and training?

- How much are you willing to invest in a new business?

If you are unsure about the answers to these questions, please take the time to think about them and, if appropriate, discuss them with your spouse or partner before you get much farther into the planning process. You don't want to get into a situation where you spend a lot of time investigating an idea, only to later discover that you can't afford to go down that path because of your financial restrictions.

Instructions: Write down your answers to the financial questions just listed:

_____

_____

_____

_____

_____

_____

_____

_____

_____

_____

An important note of caution: If you collect Social Security payments before you reach your normal retirement age (NRA) as defined by the Social Security Administration, your benefits may be reduced as a result of income you generate in your second-act career. This restriction ends once you reach your NRA. This calculation is a moving target, so please be sure to check with the Social Security Administration at www.socialsecurity.gov for the most up-to-date information regarding this provision.

THREE TIPS FROM THE FINANCIAL EXPERT

"A lot of the stress and panic I see comes from people not knowing the numbers. You'll feel better once you know where you're at."
—GALIA GICHON, founder of Down to Earth Finance
(www.downtoearthfinance.com)

The more financial flexibility you have, the greater your ability to do what you want during your semi-retirement. Here are three suggestions from an independent personal financial expert on smart ways to maximize your income during this phase of life:

1. **Renovate your semi-retirement budget to reflect your current lifestyle.** Do you still need that million-dollar life insurance policy? Is it time to stop paying your children's cell phone bills? Is the super-jumbo pack of toilet paper at Costco really still a smart purchase? You might still be spending like you've got a family to support when you could easily cut some of those expenses out of your budget.

2. **Hold off on claiming Social Security benefits as long as possible.** You can currently start claiming Social Security benefits as early as age sixty-two or as late as age seventy, but within that range, the longer you delay, the larger your monthly payments will be (you can file even later than age seventy, but your benefit amount won't be any larger). Use the online calculators provided by the Social Security Administration at www.ssa.gov/oact/anypia/index.html to run the numbers and figure out the best time to start your payments.

3. **Leverage online tools and apps to better manage your finances.** T. Rowe Price has an excellent retirement income calculator that can help you figure out what you need to live on in retirement. Galia also recommends Expenditure (www.expenditureapp.com) and MoneyBook (www.moneybookapp.com) as useful apps for setting budgets and tracking and managing your finances.

A Note about Health Insurance

What are your options for health insurance coverage if you are not yet eligible for Medicare and you will not receive health insurance retirement benefits from your employer? The answer to that question will depend on the outcome of the healthcare reform debate (with the specifics of the 2010 Affordable Care Act in flux at the time of this writing). Understanding that, here are several alternatives to consider:

- If you are covered by an employer plan, in most cases you will be eligible for COBRA, which means you can opt to continue on your employer plan for up to eighteen months (or thirty-six months for extenuating circumstances) after you terminate employment (you are responsible for paying the full premium cost, which comes as a shock to most former employees, so it's worth investigating the likely cost in advance). If you took an early retirement package, you might be able to purchase medical insurance from your employer's plan until you are eligible for Medicare.

- If your spouse or partner is still employed, you may be able to obtain benefits by enrolling in his or her plan.

- You can find more affordable group rates offered through organizations like the Freelancers Union (www.freelancersunion.org), National Association for the Self-Employed (www.nase.org), college alumni groups, and professional associations.

- If you create a small business that has a minimum of two employees, you are eligible to apply for a small business group health insurance plan. These types of plans are especially attractive if you have a preexisting condition; some states require insurance companies to offer coverage to small groups regardless of whether any person has a preexisting condition.

To more fully research your options, consult a private insurance broker or visit the website of eHealthInsurance.com.

EXERCISE: LOCATION, LOCATION, LOCATION

Where you choose to live impacts your career options. If relocation is something you are considering—whether for personal, lifestyle, or financial reasons—don't forget to factor in your second-act career as part of the equation when deciding where to live. When you relocate, it can open up access to career options that you might not have previously considered, particularly if you are able to free up capital from your home that can be applied toward your career transition.

Different towns and cities are known as "hotbeds" for different types of industries. For example:

- Beer is all the rage in Asheville, North Carolina, where they have over ten local breweries; even the bakeries and ice cream parlors carry beer-flavored products.

- Nashville, Tennessee, is well known as a home to country music, but it is also home to over 250 healthcare-related companies.

- Albany, New York, is now a popular location for the growing field of nanotechnology.

There are big benefits to setting up your career or business in the right spot. Living in an area that is filled with your peers will make it easier to find work, gain easy access to resources, and/or get a new business off the ground (beer tasting workshops, anyone?). College towns, in particular, can provide a very enriching environment for semi-retirement. They offer a compelling mix of culture, state-of-the art medical and research facilities, and easy access to reduced-rate college courses and lectures.

Relocating to a different country is also an option to consider. Countries like Costa Rica—with its high quality of life, affordable healthcare, and low housing costs—are very attractive to retirees. On a recent trip to Costa Rica, I met a woman who used to work as an attorney in the States. She opened a small café in a mountain village, where she enjoys baking and socializing with customers. To supplement her income, she works remotely several days a month on legal assignments for a firm back in the States. When the tourist season is slow, she enjoys traveling to other countries and visits with her family back home.

Even if you have no desire to relocate, be sure to take the time to appreciate the career inspiration that is right outside your door: a town that has cheap farmland might be a great spot to start an organic mushroom farm, a community with a large number of young children might be perfect for a children's birthday party service, and a town with a high percentage of seniors could be a great place to open a home healthcare agency. Once you look at your hometown as a potential career asset instead of just a place to live, your world of possibilities will expand in interesting ways.

Instructions: Jot down your thoughts about where you plan to live during semi-retirement:

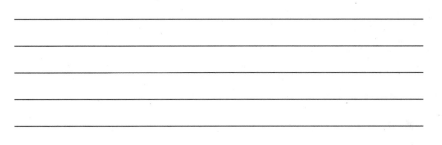

For more information about relocation options, you may find these websites valuable:

- CNN/Money, AARP, Kiplinger's, Forbes, HufffingtonPost.com, *US News & World Report*, and *CBS MoneyWatch* all publish different variations of the Best Places to Retire, Best Places to Live, and Best Places to Work lists. Go to their main website to find their most recent information.

- Topretirements.com is another site with helpful information on this topic.

MY LIFESTYLE VISION SUMMARY

In Journalism 101, college students are instructed to use the Five Ws (when, what, where, why, and who) when researching and writing their stories. Using that same formula, I'd like you to summarize the key factors you have identified as your main lifestyle goals. You can then refer back to this summary when evaluating career ideas for lifestyle fit.

Instructions: Using the exercises in this section, answer these questions:

WHEN do you want to work (hours, schedule, and so on)?

_____

_____

WHAT types of activities do you want to include/exclude in your career/life mix?

_____

_____

WHERE do you want to conduct your work activities (office setting, at home, on the road, in a small town, and so on)?

_____

_____

WHY do you want to keep working (motivators)?

_____

_____

WHO do you want to work with? Who do you want to make more time for in your professional and personal life?

_____

_____

CHAPTER TEN

Look to the Past for Clues to Your Future

Now that you have a better idea of the type of life you'd like to create during your semi-retirement, we are going to shift our focus to the career piece of the reinvention puzzle. As you reflect on and analyze your past accomplishments and experiences, you'll start to see very clear patterns emerge about what you love, what you do best, and what you find most meaningful in your life and work. Those unique patterns hold important clues to what you'll be happiest doing in the future. And once you know who you are and what is most important to you, it will be so much easier to connect with income ideas that are truly a good fit.

I know some of you may be tempted to skip this section of the book. But if you have any doubts about what you want to do next, please take the time to do the exercises in this chapter. You'll feel more at peace with your career-related decisions, if you know that you've given this process the time and attention it deserves. And you know what else? You're going to discover that this type of reflection is actually a lot of fun—you'll find yourself thinking about people, accomplishments, and events that you haven't thought about in years. It will allow you to make decisions based on a lifetime of data, as opposed to decisions that are in reaction to your most recent life experiences (for example, "I hated my last boss, so I never want to work for an employer again").

Of course, remembering forty-plus years of personal history at our age can be a bit of a challenge. I don't know about you, but I have enough trouble remembering where I put my keys, let alone what I used to like in fourth grade. So before beginning this process, I think you'll find it invaluable to take a bit of time to dust off the mental cobwebs and get the memory pipeline flowing. Here are some things you can do to help the process along:

- **Sit down with your old photo albums, family movies, scrapbooks, and yearbooks.** As you look at them, think about what they say about your past: Were you shy or the life of the party? Do you tend to be serious or silly? Who did you like to spend time with? What types of activities filled your days?

- **Clean out your closets and garage.** It's amazing how much stuff you'll find hidden away: crafts projects, sports equipment, and boxes filled with old trophies. As you go through these items, think about how your passions, hobbies, and dreams are manifested in these physical mementos.

- **Review your checkbook register and other financial documents.** What are you spending your money on? Music? Gardening? Trips? Fancy food? What we say is important doesn't always match up with how we spend our money; analyzing your spending patterns can give you important insights into your real priorities.

- **Inventory your media.** Review your collection of books, magazines, and frequented websites. Think about your television and movie viewing habits. What does your choice of media reveal about your interests?

- **Look through your personal files.** Review old resumes, performance evaluations, and other paperwork associated with your work and volunteer life. What do those files tell you about your accomplishments, interests, passions, skills, and talents?

- **Walk around your house and property.** Is your house filled with plants? Do you have a lot of artwork from different cultures? Are there collections of family photos on display? Do you have piles of sports equipment, books, or videos waiting to be enjoyed? Make note of what the items in your house say about you, your aesthetic sensibilities, and your personal priorities.

Finally, pick up the phone and call your siblings, parents, old friends, and former schoolmates to talk about your childhood and other relevant personal history. Their recollections can help fill in the blanks about your formative years.

PLAN WITH THE END IN MIND

How would you like to write your own obituary? Although this may strike you as a morbid (and premature) suggestion, it is an exercise I frequently ask my clients to do, and the results can be profound. By forcing yourself to concentrate on the big picture, you'll gain clarity about what really matters in your life and in your work. Here are some questions to ponder as you write:

- What are some professional and personal goals you have left to achieve?

- What would you do if you knew you could not fail?

- Which personality traits, quirks, and values would you like to be remembered for?

- What would you like people to say when you're gone about your contribution to your family, your community, and the greater world?

Remember, you don't need to share this obituary with anyone. Use it as a way to gain clarity about what you would like to do and achieve in the years ahead.

EXERCISE: ORGANIZE YOUR LIFE STORY WORKSHEETS

Once you've got those memories flowing, the next step in this process is to capture and organize all of that data on paper. Please segment the information into four distinct time periods as outlined:

LIFE STORY WORKSHEET #I: CHILDHOOD

It may strike you as odd to think about your childhood years when you are at or near retirement age. Trust me on this one. I can't tell you the number of times I've worked with clients who have all sorts of impressive professional accomplishments, but they end up reinventing their careers around a long-lost childhood passion. When we are children, we are free to do what we want without worry: we dance, make daisy chains, battle imaginary dragons, sing to our heart's content, and dream about becoming firemen and ballerinas. Sadly, all too often, in our efforts to be responsible adults, we lose touch with what we really love to do most, and our natural gifts and talents get crushed under the weight of all the "shoulds" and "musts" of our adult lives. Now is the time to get reacquainted with your inner child and reconnect with those long-forgotten dreams and talents. Please think about the following questions:

- What were your favorite activities and subjects during grade school?

- How did you like to spend your free time?

- What were your favorite books, movies, or television shows?

- Who were your favorite adults?

- What did you fantasize about becoming when you grew up? What did others think (or say) you would be as an adult?

Instructions: Write down your key recollections of your childhood below. It is not necessary to answer every one of these questions. Instead, use them as a starting point to inspire your writing about what you were like as a child, the types of activities you most enjoyed, and your favorite recollections of your preschool and grade school years.

_____

_____

_____

_____

_____

_____

_____

_____

_____

_____

_____

_____

_____

_____

_____

_____

_____

_____

_____

_____

LIFE STORY WORKSHEET #2:
HIGH SCHOOL AND COLLEGE

Our school years were a period of exploration, growth, and change—and also a time of conflict and anxiety as we struggled to define our place in the world. This is the life stage when most of us began to get a clearer sense of our interests, talents, and skills, both in the classroom and through our extracurricular activities. Please consider the following:

- What were your favorite subjects in high school?

- Did you have any teachers who played an influential role in your life?

- What subject(s) did you choose to focus on in college? Why?

- What were your grades like? Did you receive any special academic honors?

- Which extracurricular activities did you enjoy most?

- What profession did your friends and teachers think you'd pursue as an adult?

- How did you spend your spare time?

- Did you have any meaningful internships or part-time jobs?

- What was your social life like?

- What did you enjoy most about high school and/or college?

Instructions: On the next page, write down your recollections of your high school and college experiences. Once again, it is not necessary to answer all of the above questions individually. Use them as a prompt to inspire your writing about your most meaningful achievements, favorite things, challenges, and aspirations during your teen years.

LIFE STORY WORKSHEET #3:
THE PROFESSIONAL YEARS

Now it is time to capture information about your working life. Even if you intend to do something very different from your old (or current) line of work, it is still important to spend time thinking about your past jobs in order to identify your motivating strengths and skills. It may be helpful to take notes for each of your jobs and list the tasks, projects, and responsibilities you handled. As tempting as it is to list only your most recent or most impressive work experiences, I urge you to include details about meaningful summer or part-time jobs, as those experiences often reveal interests and talents that may not be reflected in your more "serious" jobs. Sometimes the most insignificant work experiences turn out to be the ones we enjoyed the most.

- What were your favorite jobs?

- What were your least favorite jobs?

- Which business-related skills did you most enjoy using (for example, networking, public speaking, research)? Be sure to include all of your favorite skills, not just those that were part of your official job responsibilities.

- What were your favorite work-related accomplishments?

- What kind of work environment brings out the best in you?

- Who do you want to work with? This is a big one! When I ask clients to describe the jobs they enjoyed most, do you know what they always talk about? People. The people they worked with, the people they worked for, and the people who were their clients, vendors, and colleagues. When they enjoyed the people, they loved the job; when they really didn't like the people, they inevitably disliked the job. Knowing who you most enjoy working with can help you focus in on careers that attract like-minded thinkers. Do you prefer being around women or men, children or the elderly, a homogenous group or a culturally diverse crowd, intellectuals or blue-collar types, creative or analytical personalities?

- What kinds of work-related problems and challenges do you like to solve?

Instructions: Write down your reflections, observations, and realizations about your work-related experiences, skills, and accomplishments below. Be sure to make notes about the types of people, industries, work environments, and work tasks that are your "best fit."

LIFE STORY WORKSHEET #4: PERSONAL LIFE

How you chose to spend your personal time away from work—the books you read, the friends you choose, your hobbies and travel plans—can provide illuminating insights into your strongest interests, talents, and passions.

- How do you like to spend your free time on the weekends?

- What topic(s) do you most like to talk about with your friends?

- Which subjects do you like to read about in magazines or books (for example, decorating, biking, travel, parenting, health)?

- What do you regard as your family's greatest achievement?

- Which volunteer jobs do (or did) you find most fulfilling? Why?

- Have you attended any workshops, training sessions, or continuing-education programs that you found particularly interesting?

- As a result of life experience (for example, traveling, renovating a home, cooking gourmet meals), you may have developed new interests and skills. Are there any that you consider especially meaningful or interesting?

- People gain skills and knowledge as a result of personal struggles and challenges. Note any skills or areas of expertise that you've acquired as a result of facing adversity (for example, weight loss, dealing with a learning disability).

- What role(s) do you play in your personal or family life (for example, mother hen or researcher or family events organizer or negotiator)?

Instructions: On the next page, describe your achievements, your favorite ways to spend your free time, and your greatest strengths as a friend, volunteer, and family member.

CHAPTER ELEVEN

Ask, Analyze, and Assess

Once you've had a chance to record your thoughts and feel satisfied with your responses, it is time to focus on the analysis phase of this process. Normally this is the point in most career books when you are asked to complete a series of in-depth exercises to help identify your motivating skills, accomplishments, interests, and values. Those exercises are invaluable; they work, and if you have any doubts about what you want to do or what you are good at, you should absolutely do these exercises when given the opportunity.

But we're going to take a slightly different approach here, for two reasons: First, there are already a number of excellent books and websites that cover the assessment process in far greater detail than I have space for here (more on this in just a bit). Second, I suspect that most of you already have a good sense of who you are. After all, you're no longer an eighteen-year-old kid just starting out. You've had years of experiences, accomplishments, and opportunities to discover what you love, what you do well, and what you find meaningful. My guess is that you've already had a few "aha!" moments while gathering the information for your life story worksheets. So instead of trying to persuade you to complete yet another series of exercises (which, odds are, many readers will skip), I am asking that you simply commit to answer ten key questions; then you can decide whether you need to do additional work on your own. Fair enough?

One more thing before we dig in. I want to talk for just a moment about the word "passion." I know that right about now some of you are feeling really worried that you may never find your passion. I understand. PASSION is one heck of a big word. When I hear it, I think of romance novels starring the beautiful young heroine who falls hopelessly in love with her handsome prince. Passion implies an all-consuming, "I can't sleep or think about anything else," combustive energy.

And therein lies the problem.

The word "passion" is so strong and powerful that it sets up an incredibly intimidating standard by which to evaluate your options. You might really like something. Or find it interesting. But, because you aren't totally infatuated, you dismiss it as not being good enough to work with—and over time that search for your one true passion becomes an exercise in futility.

Well, I've got news for you. Most of us aren't born with one clear passion. Sure, there are people like Michael Jordan who are blessed from birth with a clear passion for one specific career. But the majority of us mere mortals have a diverse range of interests and talents that we develop a passion for over time. I am passionate about my husband and my children, but I didn't know I would be the first day that I met them. Truth be told, I remember feeling incredibly guilty that I didn't fall in love with my first child the moment I saw her. I thought she was cute and all, but even after finally getting to hold her after nine long months, I was perfectly happy to hand her back to the nurse so I could get some sleep after a long labor. It was only over time that I fell hopelessly in love.

So if you've been feeling like you are destined for failure with this process because you can't find your one true passion, relax. Forget about passion. Focus on interests and causes you find compelling. Concentrate on the things you do really well. Think about what makes you smile. Reflect on the types of jobs you'd be proud to do and the people you would love to work with. Good enough can turn into great, intriguing can turn into enchanting, and possibilities can, and will, become passions over time. Finding your path in life is a journey. Don't let the quest for the "one and only" mythical passion derail you before you even get started.

EXERCISE: TEN KEY QUESTIONS FOR YOUR SECOND ACT

These ten questions will help give you clarity about what you like to do, what you do well, and what you find meaningful. Please refer back to your life story worksheets for help in answering these questions:

1. **Do you want to continue to do work related to your "old" profession or industry?**

   Before you answer this, let me remind you that, all things being equal, it is always easiest to do something related to what you did before (and it is the typically the best way to maximize your income). That said, I suspect that many of you would love nothing more than to shed your old career and pivot 180 degrees to a new direction. But before you make that decision final, I urge you to consider whether there isn't some piece or part of what you did before that might be worth saving.

   I leaned this lesson the hard way. After having my first child, I left my corporate human resources career to pursue a more family-friendly way to work. At the time, I fantasized about all sorts of new possibilities; one day I wanted to be a nutritionist, and the next I wanted to be in fashion. Finally, after months of patient listening, my husband grew tired of my "brainstorm of the day" and said, "Honey, I'll support whatever decision you make. But why don't you focus on something at least remotely connected to human resources? It's what you know, it's the field where you have a degree, and it is where you've invested your energy for over a decade. Isn't there *something* you can do that will build on that?"

I wasn't happy to hear that, but as much as I hated to admit it, my husband was on to something. He wasn't saying I should stay in corporate or work in human resources. He was simply suggesting that, in light of my obvious lack of a clear direction, I should consider alternatives that were in some way, shape, or form remotely connected to my professional background and education. So, recognizing that I might have been a bit hasty in my desire to start anew, I decided to figure out which pieces of my past I wanted to carry forward into my next act. And with just a little bit of analysis, it became clear that indeed there *were* parts of my career that I found quite rewarding: I enjoyed talking about jobs, I liked helping people figure out their career paths, and I was good at coaching and encouraging people. And even though the career-coaching piece had been only a small part of my former responsibilities, I learned that with additional training I could transform that part of my experience into a work-from-home business.

At the time, it was an eye-opening revelation. But now, having spent over fifteen years working with clients on their own midlife transitions, I am quite convinced that career reinvention does not have to equate to a total "do-over." There are always pieces of your previous work experience, no matter how small or seemingly insignificant, worth using as the foundational pieces of your second act.

So now let me ask you this question again, but in a slightly different way:

1. **Do you want to continue to do work related to your "old" profession or industry? And which pieces of your past work would you like to take with you into your next act?**

   When you answer this question, think in terms of your favorite work-related skills—for example, "I was great at leading meetings," or "I loved putting together budgets," or "Everyone came to me for help with technical issues." Also think about the special projects that you enjoyed, like organizing the company picnic, as well as the little things that made you happy at work, such as the opportunity to work around really smart people. Now list ten things about your past jobs (skills, projects, industry expertise, and so on) that you might consider incorporating into your next act.

_____

_____

_____

_____

_____

_____

_____

_____

_____

_____

2. **What opportunities, problems, or gaps in the market do you see?**
   Within every profession there are opportunities to create needed products, tools, and services. In your industry, you may have noticed a need for a recruiting service, a job board, an association, or a new training program. You may belong to a volunteer group that needs help with writing grants or fundraising. Or perhaps you live in a community that has a big need for a senior daycare service. What needs have you noticed? Write down at least one suggestion for a needed product or service in each of your "worlds":
   Professional life: _____
   Personal/self-improvement: _____
   Friends and family: _____

Local community: _____

Global community: _____

3. **What are your strengths?**

This question conjures up a lot of angst for many people, but this is no time for modesty. Here are some questions to get your thoughts flowing:

- What is something that you find easy to do that others find difficult?

- What are you a natural at?

- What are your special gifts or talents?

- What can't you stop yourself from doing?

- What advice or help do people ask you for?

- What type of compliments do you receive? (For example, "You are so funny," or "You should be a model," or "Why don't you have a business selling your cakes?" or "Have you ever thought of doing voiceovers?" or "You are an amazing mom.")

List your ten greatest strengths.

_____

_____

_____

_____

_____

_____

_____

_____

_____

_____

4. **What types of problems do you like to solve?**

At the end of the day, almost all businesses and careers revolve around solving problems or making things better. Think about the types of problems that interest you. Do you enjoy dealing with management challenges, piecing together puzzles, designing gardens, or helping people plan parties? Write down the types of problems that intrigue you in both your professional and personal lives.

5. What are your weaknesses?

We all have our weaknesses and it's important to acknowledge them in order to avoid problematic situations. But rather than thinking of a weakness as something you don't do well, I recommend you think of a weakness the way Marcus Buckingham describes it in his book *Find Your Strongest Life* (Thomas Nelson, 2009) as an activity that "makes you feel weak." In other words, if it bores you, frustrates you, or saps your energy, it is a weakness. Keeping that description in mind, list your weaknesses.

_____

_____

_____

_____

_____

_____

_____

_____

_____

_____

_____

_____

_____

_____

_____

_____

_____

_____

6. What do you dream about doing?

Now is the time to act on your dreams. After all, if you don't do it now, when will you? Think about the types of jobs or business ideas that you've always thought would be fun to do. Whose job would you love to have? When you look back on your career, or what you chose for your major in college, do you have buyer's remorse? If so, what would you have done differently with the benefit of hindsight? Look for the commonalities among those situations and make note of your observations.

_____

_____

_____

_____

_____

_____

_____

_____

_____

_____

_____

_____

_____

_____

_____

_____

_____

_____

7. What makes you happy?

When you're not happy, not much else matters. Think back to the times in your life when you felt most energized, creative, joyful, or "in the zone." What were you doing? Who were you with? Where were you? Think also about the little things that brighten your world, like spending time with friends, finding a great bargain, planting a vegetable garden, mastering a new song on the guitar, or planning a surprise party. List up to twenty activities that nurture your soul, make you smile, and enhance your well-being.

_____

_____

_____

_____

_____

_____

_____

_____

_____

_____

_____

_____

_____

_____ ___

_____

_____

_____

_____

8. **What do you want to spend your days talking about?**

I know this sounds basic, but sometimes there is brilliance hidden in simplicity. Do you want to talk about human potential or shoe colors? Are you more intrigued by the wildlife of Africa or the differences between sea salt and kosher salt? Make notes about the subjects, topics, and interests that you find most interesting, compelling, or meaningful.

9. **What political, global, community, or spiritual issues would you like to be involved with?**

We all have causes that we care about, and your second act can be a wonderful time to finally do something connected to your favorite causes. That said, please don't feel obligated to fill this in if nothing comes to mind.

_____

_____

_____

_____

_____

_____

_____

_____

_____

_____

_____

_____

_____

_____

_____

_____

_____

_____

_____

10. **Do you have any "easy" opportunities waiting for you?**

Sometimes we are surprisingly blind when it comes to spotting easy opportunities. A friend might be thrilled to have you join their business, your old company could be delighted to welcome you back as a consultant, or your church youth might need a group leader and you would be the perfect person. What is the "low-hanging fruit" that could, and should, be plucked from your opportunity tree? List your thoughts below.

Finally, use this space to record any additional thoughts about your career reinvention that are important to note:

Congratulations, you made it! I hope that these questions have really started you thinking and helped you to gain more clarity about your gifts, skills, and interests. But please don't be concerned if you are still are unclear about the specific jobs or careers that are your best fit. These questions are not meant to give you definitive answers about what you should do next, at least not at this point. They are intended to give you a better sense of who you are—so that when you begin to explore your options, you'll know a good fit when you see it.

If you're still feeling a bit confused as to what it is you want to do, rest assured that there are many fine career resources available to help you explore further. The easiest way to continue your exploration is by reading a few of the many wonderful books devoted to career assessment. There are hundreds of books to choose from, but here are three of my personal favorites, all of which are considered classics in their genre:

- *What Color Is Your Parachute?* by Richard Bolles (Ten Speed Press, updated yearly). If the last time you read this book was when you were in college, you are in for a pleasant surprise. *Parachute* has been revamped and updated for forty years running and is the gold standard for career changers of all ages from teens to seniors.

- *Do What You Are* by Paul D. Tieger and Barbara Barron-Tieger (Little, Brown and Company, fourth revised edition, 2007). This book helps you determine your personality type (based on the Myers-Briggs Type Indicator) and then shows you the best occupations for your type.

- *Wishcraft* by Barbara Sher with Annie Gottleib (Ballantine Books, second edition, 2003). Even though it's been a while since this book was last updated, Sher's exercises and advice are timeless. Many people describe this book as life-changing, and I agree.

Some of you may also find it beneficial to invest in working with a career professional. You can find a qualified career coach by asking for recommendations from friends or by checking the directory of the Career Thought Leaders Consortium at www.careerthoughtleaders .com. A number of universities now offer coaching services to their alumni, and you can enroll in career development workshops offered by many community colleges and continuing education programs as well. The North Carolina Center for Creative Leadership (ncccr.unca.edu/ paths-creative-retirement) offers a three-day Paths to Creative Retirement seminar several times a year on the campus of the University of North Carolina at Asheville.

Knowing what you love to do, do well, and find meaningful is critical to crafting a fulfilling second-act career. But it is not enough to focus only on what is important to you. After all, if there is no ready market for your services or products, then it will be impossible to turn your passions into profits. That is why the next step in this process is to explore ways to match your skills, talents, and motivators with real-world opportunities. Chapter twelve will teach you how to do just that.

CHAPTER TWELVE
Research the World of Possibilities

For those of you who are concerned that "doing research" sounds like an unwelcome school project, let me assure you that this is an exciting, interesting, and thought-provoking experience. Learning about new career options is going to make you feel like a kid in a career candy store: "I had no idea I could earn income doing that!" "Who knew there was a training program for that type of business?" "I can't believe I never considered this option before!" Take the time to browse, brainstorm, and savor those "aha!" moments. Even if you think you already have a pretty good idea of what you want to do next, I urge you to spend at least a little time poking around the resources included in this section. Many of you chose your careers when you were only twenty years old, and although you may have tweaked and adjusted that initial plan as your career progressed, it's probably been a long time since you've had a reason to do any serious career exploration. If you're going to make the effort to start something new, don't you owe it to yourself to familiarize yourself with the full range of possibilities?

As you learned by reading the first part of this book, the world of work has changed dramatically since we all started our careers (back in the prehistoric twentieth century). People are now earning income in ways that we never could have even imagined just a few short years ago: selling on the Internet, self-publishing books on demand, and teaching webinars online. Jobs we aspired to when we were younger have become obsolete, and new careers—like virtual assistants, app designers, social media consultants, and bloggers—have filled the void.

How do you learn about these new paths? By paying attention—reading, watching informational videos, and making it a point to be an "active learner." By engaging with people—talking, asking questions, and doing a lot of listening. By "doing"—taking classes, interning, volunteering, and traveling. Each action you take becomes its own mini-research project, and over time you'll find yourself becoming an expert about a whole new world of exciting career options.

So if you're ready to do some exploring, here are sixteen different ideas that will help you as you continue this process on your own going forward.

HELPFUL TOOLS, STRATEGIES, AND RESOURCES

1. **Consult your colleagues.** Here is an obvious but sometimes overlooked career research strategy: If you want to do something connected to your former profession, but you're trying to figure out how to do it on a more flexible basis, there is no better way to get ideas than to talk with your industry colleagues. They know you, and they know the industry. And assuming the two of you are close in age, they may be actively thinking about the very same issues themselves. This is a case where two heads are indeed better than one; together you can brainstorm ideas, discuss training programs, and investigate ways to create multiple income streams around needed products or services.

2. **Explore industry associations.** Industry associations are a fabulous resource for learning more about career options within any

industry (and believe me when I say there is an association for virtually every type of career and business that you can imagine). You can benefit from their offerings in a number of different ways:

- **Visit their websites.** This is the fastest way to get familiar with the association's products, services, members, and training programs. To locate your industry association, consult the *Gale Encyclopedia of Associations* (you can find the book in the reference section of your library), or simply do a Google search using the appropriate keywords, such as "personal fitness association."

- **Read your industry trade journal or newsletter.** Larger industries produce trade journals and magazines; smaller ones tend to have newsletters, many of which are accessible online. In either format, these publications can be an excellent source of ideas and inspiration.

- **Get involved.** National associations and trade groups have local chapters that host networking and educational meetings. Attending a meeting is a smart way to meet people and learn about career-related opportunities. Volunteering to help the group in a leadership capacity is also a great way to make important connections, form partnerships, and raise your profile among your peers.

- **Attend their annual conference.** Conferences are a terrific place to hear industry leaders speak, make new friends, and learn about new vendors, products, and services for people in your profession. Several of the people I interviewed for this book said that conferences played an important role in their business success, and they found them to be well worth the price of admission. If you can't afford to fly to a conference, consider attending a one-day workshop in your local area or take advantage of online webinars instead.

- **Explore their training programs and options for certifications.** Trade and association groups sponsor a wide range of educational and certification opportunities, many of which are exclusive to their membership.

3. **Consult the college catalogs (even if you don't plan to go back to school).** Hands down, one of my favorite ways to research career options is to read through the programs and classes offered by colleges and universities. I discovered the value of "catalog surfing" when going through my own career reinvention many years ago. At the time, I was working in corporate human resources and was desperate to figure out a way to transition into a more lifestyle-friendly career; I really wanted to get out of a corporate environment, but I didn't know what else to do. So I went to the library to research advanced degree programs for people with a background in psychology, sat down with the *Peterson's Guide to the Colleges*, and, purely by chance, stumbled upon a master's degree program in career development. After reading the description of the courses, I was convinced that their program was a perfect fit with my background and interests. Many of my clients have experienced the same "luck" by scrolling through college catalogs and websites to uncover exciting variations of careers that they didn't even know existed.

Even if you don't plan on going back to school, it's worthwhile to check the school catalogs and continuing education offerings, just to see what courses are being offered. Their catalogs can provide you with ideas about emerging fields and "hot" careers, as well as information about certificate programs and certification options. Two of my favorite resources for researching educational programs are *US News & World Report* (www.usnews.com) and Peterson's Guides (www.petersons.com). When you look for college programs, be sure to also check with community colleges and continuing education programs, which typically have classes that are great for people who want to start their own businesses. For example, my local continuing education program offers classes that include How to Make Money as a Photographer, How to Earn Money as a Voiceover Professional, and How to Become an Event Planner.

4. **Check out the "career idea" books.** There are hundreds, if not thousands, of books that can help you research a great new career. Some of the books, such as this one, provide mini-snapshots of a variety of careers; other titles feature detailed step-by-step advice on a specific career or business idea, such as how to earn an income online, how to make money selling gourmet products, or how to flourish as a consultant. In addition to locating these books at brick-and-mortar bookstores or on online sites, many industry association websites have online bookstores that sell industry-specific books and other informational products.

5. **Look at the US Department of Labor sites.** It may surprise you to learn that our federal government funds much of the career data that is produced in this country, but they do, and their sites are excellent. I consider them the equivalent of the *Encyclopedia Britannica* of the careers world: chock full of more information than one person could possibly digest, and a tremendous resource when you need to explore career possibilities. Here are four of their most helpful websites:

- **America's CareerInfoNet (www.acinet.org).** On this mega-site you can research wages and employment trends, occupational requirements, and state-by-state labor market conditions and take advantage of the most extensive career resource library online.

- **My Skills, My Future (www.myskillsmyfuture.org).** This site asks you to input your old job title; it then responds with suggestions of jobs that match your background and skills. It is a very helpful tool for generating ideas that you might not have previously considered.

- **O*NET Resource Center (www.onetcenter.org).** The O*NET program is the nation's primary source of occupational information, with a robust database of hundreds of occupations. This resource is so extensive that they have now created the O*NET Academy (www.onetacademy.org), a site that teaches how to maximize your use of O*NET's capabilities and resources (and of course, all the training is provided free of charge).

- **The Occupational Outlook Handbook (OOH) (www.bls.gov/ooh).** The OOH, updated every two years by the Bureau of Labor Statistics, provides detailed information about hundreds of careers. As the name implies, this is a great resource to help you both learn about different professions and decide which industries should have strong growth potential in the future. It is one of my all-time favorite resources.

6. **Visit career portal sites.** In addition to the sites sponsored by the government, there are numerous private and university sites that offer a helpful overview of careers. Here are three worth mentioning:

- **MyPlan.com (www.myplan.com).** This site features comprehensive information about over nine hundred careers. You can read career profiles, watch videos about five hundred different careers and industries, and learn about the types of people who typically go into each career. Although this site is geared toward college students, it is still worth a visit, no matter your age.

- **The Riley Guide (www.rileyguide.com).** The Riley Guide was one of the first major career research sites on the Web, and it remains a favorite among career professionals. Don't be put off by its low-tech appearance; what it lacks in glitz, it makes up for in quality, scope, and content.

- **eHow (www.ehow.com/careers).** This site has short videos about how to get started in a number of careers and entrepreneurial ventures. Their current roster of offerings includes How to Earn Passive Income Writing, What to Put into a Modeling Portfolio, and How to Become a Stockbroker.

7. **Leverage the social media sites.** All three of the big players in the social media sphere—Twitter, LinkedIn, and Facebook—are helpful tools for people looking to research business and career ideas. Learning how to use all the many features of these sites takes some focus, but I think you'll find it to be a worthwhile investment of your time. Here are five easy ways to engage social media as part of your career research endeavors:

- **Post a question on Facebook, tweet a question on Twitter, or submit a question to your LinkedIn network.** Keep your request for information short, simple, and specific. For example, "I am exploring career opportunities as a food writer. Looking for recommendations of good training programs." You never know who might be able to provide you with a helpful tip or suggestion.

- **Follow groups on Facebook.** There are thousands of niche industry groups on Facebook that you can follow. Identify a few that might be beneficial and connect with them to automatically receive their news feeds and updates.

- **Follow industry "gurus" on Twitter.** Every industry has its star performers, and these days many of those people are sharing their thoughts on Twitter. Sign up for a Twitter account at Twitter.com (don't worry, you don't need to tweet in order to maintain your account) and then find interesting people to follow by using search directories like Twellow.com ("the Twitter Yellow Pages") or WeFollow.com.

- **Join an industry-related group on LinkedIn.** Go to the "Groups" tab and search to find groups that you would like to join. Some groups have restricted membership, but most are open to all interested parties. Once you're a member of a group, sign up to receive automated updates so you'll be kept informed about relevant events, training programs, and news on a regular basis. Participate in the group discussions—it's a great way to meet people and build relationships in your new field of interest.

- **Search for jobs on LinkedIn or Twitter.** Even if you are not actively seeking a job, reviewing the job postings on LinkedIn or Twitter can provide you with helpful information about the variety of jobs available in your field of interest.

8. **Learn from the job listings.** One of the simplest ways to research careers is to scan the job boards (even if you are not actively looking for a job); you'll learn about the skills, educational requirements, salary ranges, and opportunities for lots of different careers. There are thousands of job boards on the Internet where you could do research; here are five of the best:

- **Job board aggregators.** There are now several sites that pull millions of job listings from other job boards and post them in one central location. Sites like Indeed.com, SimplyHired.com, and Guru.com (for freelancers) are great first stops for anyone doing career research via the job boards.

- **Industry niche sites.** Once you have focused on an industry, it can be helpful to look through the job listings on industry-specific boards like Mediabistro.com (media industry) or Idealist.org (nonprofits). To find a job board in your industry, do a Google search using appropriate keywords or consult Job-hunt.org or Rileyguide.com.

- **Associations.** Almost all associations now host some sort of job board or careers page on their websites.

- **Company sites.** Companies, universities, and nonprofits almost always list job openings on their websites.

- **Craigslist.org.** Entrepreneurs and small businesses love to list their job openings and contract work opportunities on Craigslist.org. It is the go-to site for locating unique entrepreneurial job and freelance opportunities.

9. **Explore Alltop.com.** If you're one of those people who enjoys browsing the mega-magazine displays at airports, then you're going to love Alltop, which bills itself as the online "magazine rack" of the Web. Alltop.com helps you quickly locate the highest-quality information on hundreds of interesting and diverse topics ranging from business to cheese to sports. They compile the latest stories and headlines from their hand-picked list of blogs and websites, and because they feature only stories from trusted sources, their results are free of the junk you normally need to sift through on other search engines.

10. **Visit YouTube.com.** YouTube is the go-to destination for informational videos about thousands of careers and entrepreneurial options. It's easy, it's free, and all you need to do is go to the site (or find the videos on Google.com) and input the relevant search words (for example, "Green Careers" or "Executive Coaching Business" or "How to Become a Makeup Artist"); with any luck, your search will return at least a few relevant videos. Of course, you'll need to be careful to look for videos from credible sources, because anyone can post a video on YouTube.com.

11. **Read business magazines and newspapers.** Although most people read business magazines and newspapers to get financial information and business news, these can also be a good source of inspiration, resources, and ideas for career changers. The *Wall Street Journal, Fortune, Fast Company, US News & World Report, Kiplinger's, AARP,* and *Money,* along with their related websites,

all feature stories about hot careers, great business ideas, and profiles of successful entrepreneurs.

12. **Browse through popular and niche magazines.** Most of us read magazines for fun and diversion, but they can also be a surprisingly helpful source of ideas about new career paths and business opportunities. Here are some tips for maximizing the use of magazines in your career research:

- **Learn about trends.** Magazines like *Inc.* and *Entrepreneur* routinely print articles about small business trends. Every year *Entrepreneur* publishes their predictions for the hottest business trends likely to emerge in the coming year, along with suggestions on how to capitalize on those trends.

- **Read niche publications.** Did you ever notice how many magazines are targeted to specific hobbies and niche interests? There are magazines for pet lovers, chocolate fanatics, golfers, parents, crafters, and wine enthusiasts (just to name a few). Those magazines focus their coverage on the people, businesses, and products associated with those niches—highly specific information that can be difficult to find elsewhere.

- **Get inspired by profiles.** Many magazines have columns showcasing inspirational stories about entrepreneurs, career changers, and business leaders. Reading their stories will help you discover innovative ways to turn your passions into profits.

- **Pay attention to advertisements.** The advertisements in niche magazines feature information about industry-specific training programs, franchises, and business opportunities that might be a good match for your needs. The advertisements are also a good way to learn about clever niche-related products, gizmos, and inventions that might inspire your thinking and help you innovate new product offerings of your own.

13. **Throw an idea party.** I first learned of "idea parties" from career counselor and best-selling author Barbara Sher in her book *Live the Life You Love* (Dell, 1996). Sher defines an idea party as "a potluck dinner where you invite people into your home for the express purpose of sitting down with a plate of good food and brainstorming on your particular problem." It's a fun evening of camaraderie and conversation that can lead to a new direction for your career.

   This idea makes perfect sense. After all, you turn to your friends if you need help choosing a paint color or finding the best hip surgeon, so why not enlist their aid with your career reinvention? They can help you brainstorm ideas, find resources, and think about options that you might never consider on your own. Before you send out the invitations, it is important to do your own preliminary research and personal assessment. After all, you can't expect your friends to solve your "What should I be when I grow up?" dilemma for you; that is up to you. But the idea party can help generate specific ideas, resources, and strategies that will move you closer to your goals. Here are some tips on how to create a successful idea party:

   - **The purpose of an idea party is to generate ideas through an open brainstorming session.** You'll want to invite people who are good outside-the-box thinkers, supportive personalities, and creative thinkers; leave the "Debbie Downers" home. And feel free to ask friends to invite someone you don't know. The input of people outside your normal circle of influence could prove to be extremely enlightening.

   - **Make it easy for your friends to help you by asking for specific information and resources.** The more specific you are, the greater the likelihood that your friends will be able to respond in concrete and meaningful ways.

- **Serve good food and drink.** It will make your guests feel appreciated.

- **Remember to send each of your guests a thank-you note.** This may seem like an unnecessary formality, but it will be very much appreciated.

Finally, don't forget to pay it forward. Let your friends know that you'll be there for them when they need your help and assistance down the road.

14. **Get inspired by second-act career stories.** Reading and hearing motivational stories is, well, inspiring. There are a number of excellent sites on the Web that have motivational stories about people over forty reinventing their careers. In no particular order, here are some that you may find quite useful:

    - **AARP (www.aarp.org/work/working-after-retirement).** AARP has built a robust work and retirement section on their website, complete with recommendations of work-from-home and part-time employment ideas. AARP's "Your Life Calling" with Jane Pauley is an award-winning TV series on the NBC *TODAY* show highlighting people age fifty-plus who are reinventing themselves in new and different ways. You can visit www.aarp.org/your_life_calling/ for more information on the TV series or, for a full archive of stories, http://www.aarp.org/personal-growth/transitions/ylc_index.

    - **Next Avenue (www.nextavenue.org).** The Public Broadcasting Service (PBS) launched this site in May 2012 to help "grown-ups keep growing"; it features numerous articles and profiles focused on work and purpose.

    - **Huff/Post50 (www.huffingtonpost.com/50).** All of the content on this Huffington Post site is geared for the baby boomer generation and includes many posts related to career and reinvention topics.

- **Encore.org (www.encore.org).** Encore.org is for people interested in encore careers—jobs that combine personal meaning, income, and social impact. Their site is an excellent resource for people who want to create their second acts in the non-profit world.

- **More.com (www.more.com).** The website for *More* magazine has many stories about career reinvention for women over forty. Although the magazine is intended for women, the stories are equally useful for men.

- **TED (Technology, Entertainment, Design) (www.ted.com).** If you're not already familiar with TED, you should check out their TED Talk videos that feature over one thousand of the world's most inspirational speakers on a wide range of topics. They are both educational and awe inspiring. This site is one of my personal favorites.

15. **Gaze into the crystal ball.** The world of work is changing rapidly. What is hot today may be obsolete tomorrow. Take the time to learn about emerging trends and predictions for the future. That futuristic orientation will serve you well and will inspire you to think more broadly about potential business ideas and career possibilities. Here are some sites to help do just that:

    - **World Future Society (www.wfs.org).** The World Future Society is an organization dedicated to exploring the future. Their magazine, *The Futurist*, is sold on newsstands, and their website is a great resource about future trends and predictions.

    - **Faith Popcorn (www.faithpopcorn.com).** Faith Popcorn is a renowned futurist and founder and CEO of the marketing consulting firm, BrainReserve. Most of the information on her site is geared toward corporate clients, but if you look carefully, you'll find several free reports summarizing her key trends and predictions.

- **Springwise.com (www.springwise.com).** Springwise.com's tag line is "Your essential fix of entrepreneurial ideas." Their site features promising business venture ideas and concepts—a fantastic resource for entrepreneurs looking for the "next big thing."

- **Trendwatching.com (www.trendwatching.com).** Trendwatching.com reports on emerging consumer trends, insights, and innovations. You can sign up for their free monthly trend reports.

- **Trend Hunter (www.trendhunter.com).** This is the site for people interested in trends in fashion, pop culture, art and design, social media and technology. As of this writing, this site was averaging over thirty-five million views a month— now that is one trendy site!

- **Mashable (mashable.com).** Although not technically a trend site, Mashable is the largest independent online news site dedicated to covering digital culture, social media, and technology—an outstanding resource for all things tech.

16. **Conduct informational interviews.** There is a limit to what you can learn about prospective careers from just reading and research. At some point, you'll need to turn off the computer, close the books, and start talking with people who are doing what you'd like to do. Speaking with other people is the single most effective way to learn about new career options, and conducting informational interviews will help you get a real-life perspective of what it's like to work in a specific job or business, before you invest time or money transitioning into a new career.

    Some people are reluctant to ask for informational interviews, fearing that they might appear foolish (especially if the person they are contacting is much younger) or that their request will be viewed as an imposition. That is understandable, but the reality is that most people will be flattered by your request and will want to help—most people love to talk about themselves! You can ease into this process by first contacting your inner circle of friends, neighbors, and relatives, and then expanding your outreach to their extended network of contacts. Here are some sample questions to ask during your informational interview:

- What do you enjoy most about your job?

- What are the most frustrating aspects of your job?

- What are the most important characteristics for success in this career?

- What training should I pursue to make myself more marketable in this field?

- Which professional associations would you recommend I join?

- What are the challenges, trends, and opportunities in this profession?

- Are there good options for freelance or consulting work within this industry?

- Which magazines, journals, or websites do you recommend?

- Are there opportunities for flexible work arrangements?

- Is there someone else you recommend I speak to?

- May I use your name in making the introduction?

Of course, you should always follow up your meetings with a thank-you note (these days e-mail notes are sufficient, but a handwritten note is still a lovely surprise). And do be sure to circle back with your contacts and let them know about your progress as your plans evolve.

CHAPTER THIRTEEN

Try It Out!

After you've identified some intriguing career or home-based business options, and have gathered useful data about each choice, the next step is to assess those options for "fit" by trying them out. Evaluating each option against your unique package of skills, interests, experience, and values will help you answer the question, "Is this a good fit?" Here are some key questions to ask as you weigh your choices:

- Does this career or business take advantage of my experience and background?

- Is this a good match for my motivating skills, interests, and values?

- Is this a good fit with my lifestyle and salary objectives?

- What additional training, certification, or licensing do I need to get started in this field? Are there schools around me that offer the training I need? If not, are there online options for education? Am I willing to invest in this additional education? Are there industry or entrepreneurial associations I should join to help build my skills and contacts in this field?

- Do I have the time, money, and energy to prepare myself for success in this job? If not, are there alternative careers in this industry that might be a more suitable fit?

Lots of potential career or home-based business ideas will sound exciting when you read about them, but you won't really know whether they are a good choice until you've had a chance to actually test them out. Fortunately there are several low-risk ways to do that:

Volunteer. Volunteering is a win-win for all involved; the organization benefits from your efforts, and you gain experience that you can leverage as part of your career reinvention. To maximize the benefits, be strategic about where and how you choose to volunteer. For example, if you're thinking about transitioning into healthcare, you should try to find opportunities to volunteer in a healthcare setting that is focused on your specific field of interest; if you're considering a pet-related business, you can volunteer at a vet's office or animal shelter.

Pursue a part-time or freelance job. Sometimes it makes sense to take on a small part-time job as a way to learn about a new industry. For example, if you're interested in selling your prized brownies online, but you have no real experience in the food industry, you might want to work for a local bakery to get a taste of life in the baking world. Or if you're thinking of getting a certificate in health coaching, you might want to get a part-time job as a meeting leader with Weight Watchers to determine whether you like working in that industry. Although working in a lower-level job may require a bit of an ego adjustment, you will enjoy them more if you think of them as an apprenticeship and research opportunity.

Intern. There once was a time when only college students took advantage of internships. But in today's competitive global market, people of all ages have discovered the value of internships as a way to evaluate and build new career paths. To learn more about how to locate an internship in your field of interest, consult Internship.com or the Guide to Internships on About.com at www.internships.about.com.

Indulge in a vocation vacation. How would you like a chance to work alongside a winemaker in Napa, a director on Broadway, or an alpaca rancher in Oregon? VocationVacations is a service that offers you the chance to test-drive your target career while being mentored by a professional in that field. To learn more, be sure to check out their site at www.vocationvacations.com.

Take a class. Taking a class, even if it is just a short workshop or seminar, will provide you with an opportunity to evaluate your interest in potential career and business options, learn new skills, and meet new people who can stimulate your thinking about your future career plans. Adult education is a big business these days, and there are more opportunities than ever to indulge in lifelong learning. As you may have gathered while reading part one of this book, there is a training program for every business imaginable, from dog walking to jewelry making (heck, I even came across a training program for hot dog vendors!). That said, you'd be wise to exercise caution if you plan to invest in a certificate program, boot camp, or "university" run by an independent entrepreneur. The quality and legitimacy of those programs vary considerably, so ask lots of questions, do your homework, and always check around before investing your hard-earned dollars.

Of course, enrolling to study with an established school or college is generally a safer bet. There are an increasing number of online programs being offered by, or in conjunction with, leading colleges and universities, and some of these programs are specifically targeting the second-act market. One example is Empowered.com, an online educator that offers certificate programs in "hot" fields such as patient advocacy, college counseling, and financial planning. Their courses are taught by the faculty of UCLA's extension program using iPad technology (all students who enroll in their year-long certificate programs receive an iPad), and students are also provided access to extensive career guidance services to help them as they plan for their next acts.

Here are several more reasons why now might be the prime time for you to return to school:

- **Tuition waivers.** More than half of accredited degree-granting educational institutions offer tuition waivers or discounts for older adults. Many colleges allow people age sixty or older to audit classes (meaning you can attend lectures without the homework and exams). Although you won't be eligible for college credit, you will enjoy the same learning opportunity as your twenty-something classmates.

- **Low-cost community colleges.** Community colleges provide a very affordable way to continue your education, and they offer valuable certification and trade-specific vocational training options. Some community colleges also participate in the Plus 50 Initiative, a national program that helps community colleges create or expand "ageless learning" programs and life transition counseling services for people over fifty. To find a participating community college near you, consult www.aacc.nche.edu/pages/ccfinder.aspx.

- **Classes for people over fifty.** A growing number of colleges are offering continuing education classes geared specifically for older adults. Worth a special mention is the network of Osher Lifelong Learning Institutes, located at approximately 120 colleges and universities throughout the United States, including schools like Duke, Johns Hopkins, and Vanderbilt. Osher provides a robust calendar of adult learning opportunities with the emphasis on learning for the joy of learning—without the burden of homework and exams. Fees vary considerably by location, but they tend to be very affordable, especially when compared to traditional college classes.

- **Residential campus learning communities.** A growing number of colleges, including Dartmouth College and the University of Florida at Gainesville, have retirement communities that are located on or near the campus. Residents of these communities are often allowed to attend classes for free (and may be entitled to other benefits, like tickets to college sporting events).

- **Opportunities to learn while traveling.** Road Scholar (formerly known as Elderhostel) is a nonprofit organization offering a wide variety of experiential and adventure learning opportunities. Road Scholar (www.roadscholar.org) works in partnership with non-profit educational institutions, such as museums and universities, to provide high-quality, college-level educational programs and classes.

Conclusion: Some Final Tips on Creating Your Second-Act Career

As we come to the end of this journey, I want to leave you with some thoughts on how to get the most out of this reinvention process as you move forward on your own. In some ways, creating a new career works a bit like planting a garden: you ready the soil, plant the seeds, water regularly, wait patiently, and over time new growth emerges from the ground up. The same is true when people reinvent their careers: it takes a bit of work to get things rolling, but if you invest the time to create fertile growing conditions, then you get to enjoy a bountiful harvest. So before concluding, here are some tips on the best ways to ensure optimal growing conditions for your second act:

- **Budget for success.** Career transitions take time, so plan your finances accordingly. Most experts advise that you set aside at least eighteen months of living expenses to tide you over as you go through the process of planning, training for, and implementing a new career plan. As early as you can, start paying down outstanding debts, downsize your lifestyle if necessary, and plan to take advantage of any employer tuition reimbursement plans and training programs before leaving your job.

- **Set a reinvention research and development "R&D" budget.** Put aside some funds to invest in your personal R&D activities. It doesn't need to be much, but knowing that you have earmarked funds for your personal development will make it more likely that you'll take advantage of learning opportunities as they surface. That money can then be used—guilt free—for classes, retreats, books, and other training that could significantly accelerate the speed of your progress.

- **Keep a reinvention journal.** Writing things down will help you capture your thoughts and remember important facts. It will also help create clarity during a sometimes confusing transition; it is remarkable how much easier it is to analyze issues when you write them down instead of simply trying to think them through.

- **Schedule your reinvention projects on a calendar.** Scheduling these activities on your calendar will make your commitment real. I ask my clients (most of whom fall into the overworked and overwhelmed category) to use this time-management technique, and the ones who put it into practice, love it. It gives them a structure, workable boundaries, and improved productivity.

- **Buddy up for success.** This process is so much more enjoyable— and effective—when you share it with others. Ideally your spouse or life partner will act as your most enthusiastic ally and cheer-leader. But if not, buddy up with a trusted friend or group of people who are actively in the process of building their second-act careers. Remember, a great support system turns possibilities into probabilities—and dreams into reality.

- **Expect resistance.** Change is uncomfortable; human beings are hardwired to resist venturing into the unknown. Know that there will be times when you will be stuck at a crossroads or frustrated by indecision. And it's not just *you* who may be feeling fear.

Family and friends may be scared by the changes as well ("You want to do *what*?"), and they may not always be as supportive or encouraging as you'd wish. Be patient, stay calm, keep communicating, and give everyone time to adjust.

- **Don't force it.** Sometimes taking a break will speed up your progress more than trying to force your way to an answer. I periodically remind my husband of this when he works on the *New York Times* crossword puzzle. He always starts the puzzle with great enthusiasm, but as the clues become more challenging and his progress slows, he grows more frustrated. Ironically when he does force himself to take a break, when he returns to the puzzle he is able to finish it with relative ease. Walking away from the puzzle gives him a chance to relax, refresh, and look at the clues with fresh eyes. Crafting a new career is a bit like solving a crossword puzzle. Sometimes your breakthrough moments will happen when you least expect them, so be willing to step away and take a break in order to gain some needed perspective.

- **Reinvention is going to take the time it takes, so start early!** I have yet to see a career reinvention unfold exactly according to schedule. It's a process that can take months, or even years, to fully evolve, and no matter how well you plan, there will be unexpected twists and turns. You'll get excited about an idea, begin to research options, and discover that you need to take a few classes before you can begin to move forward with your plans. Or you'll come down with the flu. Or the doctor says you may soon be needing a knee replacement. Or—well, you get the idea. Bottom line is that you should expect the unexpected, so the sooner you begin the reinvention process, the better off you'll be.

The path to a second-act career is rarely a straight line; it is a meandering journey, on which you are propelled by patience, determination, and a willingness to adapt as circumstances change. It is characterized by failure, doubt, and false starts, but it is also graced by generosity, moments of clarity, and serendipity. Career reinvention is not one seamless transition, but a series of smaller actions that link together to create lasting change. You'll have a conversation—that leads to an introduction to a new person—who leads you to a fun part-time job; or you'll read a book—that gets you excited about taking a course—that leads to learning a new skill—that enables you to start a new business.

You never know where or when or how reinvention magic will happen. But it will. So relax, and remember to have fun as you go on your way. And as you proceed, keep in mind this thought from Gracie Cavnar, the founder of Recipe for Success, who says, "I know it sounds trite, and people have been saying it for decades, but find your bliss. Something you love so much that you can't wait when you wake in the morning to get started. Now is the time to do that. Life is what is happening while you are waiting for it."

What are you waiting for? Now is your time. The curtain is going up, and your second act is about to begin. Godspeed, and enjoy the journey.

Resources

Websites change constantly, so if you don't find a resource under the suggested URL, do a keyword search to find similar resources. Also, please be sure to sign up for my newsletter at MyLifestyleCareer.com to receive automatic updates about additional great resources for creating a lifestyle-friendly career.

Advice for People Wanting to Work Without a 9-to-5 Job

I turn to this list of experts and authors whenever I am looking for new ideas, insights, and resources about flexible work. They represent a wide range of ages, values, and sensibilities (some of which might not match your own), but putting value and age differences aside, I think you'll learn a lot from their blogs, books, classes, and other informational offerings.

- Barbara Winter (www.joyfullyjobless.com)

- Chris Guillebeau (www.chrisguillebeau.com)

- Dan Miller (www.48days.com)

- Jonathan Fields (www.jonathanfields.com)

- Jonathan Mead (www.paidtoexist.com)

- Kerry Hannon (www.kerryhannon.com)

- Michael Hyatt (www.michaelhyatt.com)

- Natalie Sisson (www.suitcaseentrepreneur.com)

- Pamela Slim (www.escapefromcubliclenation.com)

- Scott Dinsmore (www.liveyourlegend.net)

- Sean Ogle (www.seanogle.com)

- Valerie Young (www.changingcourse.com)

Online Career Tests

While I am not a big fan of online career tests in general, as I think many are designed to deliver quick answers as opposed to truly useful insights, they can be helpful if you use them in conjunction with other tools. Here are some you might find useful:

- Myers Briggs Type Indicator (MBTI) (www.myersbriggs.org)

- Strong Life Test (www.stronglifetest.com)

- Career Key (www.careerkey.org/asp/your_personality/take_test.html)

- Questionnaire Center of the Positive Psychology program at the University of Pennsylvania (www.authentichappiness.sas.upenn .edu/questionnaires.aspx). Although these are not technically career tests, they will help you gain insight into your strengths, motivators, and happiness drivers.

Entrepreneurial Resources

- BizStarters (www.bizstarters.com). Advice for entrepreneurs over fifty.

- *Entrepreneur* magazine (www.entrepreneur.com).

- FabJob Guides (www.fabjob.com). Step-by-step guides to starting your own business.

- Freelancers Academy (www.freelancersacademy.com). Site for both new and experienced freelancers.

- Open Forum (www.openforum.com). A wealth of resources for small business owners.

- PivotPlanet (www.pivotplanet.com). One-on-one video or voice sessions with expert advisors working in hundreds of different fields (a fee applies).

- Rise to the Top (www.risetothetop.com). Video interviews with entrepreneurs.

- Small Business Administration (www.sba.gov). Government-sponsored site brimming with information and resources for entrepreneurs.

- SmartBrief on Entrepreneurs (www.smartbrief.com). Free e-mail newsletter.

- Spark and Hustle (www.sparkandhustle.com). Regional conferences for female entrepreneurs.

Job Search Sites Specifically for People 50+

- BoomerJobs (www.boomerjobs.com)

- RetirementJobs (www.retirementjobs.com)

- Seniors4Hire (www.seniors4hire.org)

- Workforce50 (www.workforce50.com)

- Work Reimagined (www.workreimagined.aarp.org/#about)

About the Author

Nancy Collamer, MS, is a career coach, author, and speaker who is an expert at helping people create lifestyle-friendly careers. In private practice since 1996, Nancy gained national prominence as the Career Transitions columnist for Oxygen Media and as the founder of the popular websites MyLifestyleCareer.com and Jobsandmoms.com. She holds a MS in career development from the College of New Rochelle and a BA in psychology from the University of North Carolina at Chapel Hill.

Her advice has been featured in numerous media outlets, including *NBC Nightly News*; the *New York Times*; *CNN*; the *Wall Street Journal*; *Redbook*; *Ladies' Home Journal*; *More*; *O, The Oprah Magazine*; and *Fortune*. She has written columns about lifestyle-friendly careers for a number of major websites, including AARP.org, MariaShriver.com, NextAvenue.org, and Job-Hunt.org. Nancy enjoys sharing her expertise with live audiences, both large and small, and has spoken at venues ranging from Harvard Business School to the California Governor and First Lady's Conference on Women.

When not at work, Nancy loves spending time at her home in Old Greenwich, Connecticut, with her husband, Joel, their two daughters, Danielle and Juliana, and her one-eyed cat, Annabelle. She is a rabid UNC Tar Heel basketball fan and a proud card-carrying member of AARP.

To Contact Nancy

I really want to hear your success stories and your own "lessons learned", so please don't be a stranger! There are several ways to connect with me:

Visit MyLifestyleCareer.com: You'll find lots of information, profiles, and resources to help you as you craft your semi-retirement career. Be sure to sign up for my updates on the site.

Connect on Twitter @NancyCollamer

Follow me on Facebook at www.facebook.com/mylifestylecareer

Speaking engagements: I adore speaking to audiences, both large and small, about semi-retirement careers, and I always enjoy the opportunity to share inspirational stories, actionable strategies, and little-known resources. Most of all, I love making those lightbulb moments happen! To inquire about booking a speaking engagement, e-mail me at njcollamer@gmail.com.

Consulting/coaching: If you're interested in hiring me as a coach who can help jump-start your semi-retirement plans, I'd love to hear from you. Best way to reach me is by e-mail at njcollamer@gmail.com.

Index

More Career Guidance from TEN SPEED PRESS

What Color Is Your Parachute?
Guide to Job-Hunting Online
6TH EDITION
by Mark Emery Bolles and
Richard Nelson Bolles
$12.99 paperback (Canada: $14.99)
ISBN: 978-1-60774-033-9
eBook ISBN: 978-1-60774-042-1

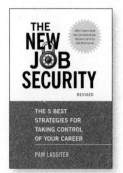

The New Job Security
The 5 Best Strategies for Taking
Control of Your Career
REVISED
by Pam Lassiter
$14.99 paperback (Canada: $16.99)
ISBN: 978-1-58008-377-5
eBook ISBN: 978-1-58008-673-8

The 2-Hour Job Search
Using Technology to Get the
Right Job Faster
by Steve Dalton
$12.99 paperback (Canada: $14.99)
ISBN: 978-1-60774-170-1
eBook ISBN: 978-1-60774-171-8

Strategies for Successful
Career Change
Finding Your Very Best Next Work Life
by Martha E. Mangelsdorf
$16.99 paperback (Canada: $21.99)
ISBN 978-1-58008-824-4
eBook ISBN: 978-0-307-76854-4

Available from Ten Speed Press wherever books are sold.

www.tenspeed.com